OTHER BOOKS AND CDs BY DENNIS JERNIGAN —

Books:
Giant Killer
> a book for those who desire freedom from bondage —
> Dennis Jernigan's personal story of how he came
> to know freedom from homosexuality

Help Me to Remember
> a book for those who grieve or for those who desire to
> minister to those who grieve

This is My Destiny
> a study of our identity in Christ

A Mystery of Majesty
> a study of the great majesty of God

CDs:
I Surrender
This is My Destiny
Giant Killers
Hands Lifted High
> a collection of Dennis Jernigan singing his
> music with many of today's top Christian recording artists
> such as Natalie Grant, Twila Paris, Ron Kenoly, Charlie
> Hall, Rebecca St. James, Annie Herring, Matthew Ward,
> Russ Taff, Watermark, Charmaine, Jeff Deyo, Alvin
> Slaughter, Russ Taff, and Travis Cottrell

Dennis has recorded more than 25 albums of original music used by the body of
Christ around the world. For more information:

Shepherd's Heart Music, Inc. — 1-800-877-0406
3201 N. 74th St. West
Muskogee, Oklahoma 74401

www.dennisjernigan.com

OUR PURPOSE AT SHEPHERD'S HEART MUSIC PUBLISHING IS TO:

• *Lead hurting, wounded* people to health and life through faith in Jesus Christ
• *Lead people* into a deeper understanding of their identity through faith in Jesus Christ
• *Lead people* to freedom from the bondage of sin
• *To make* Christ known

This Is My Destiny © 1999 by Dennis Jernigan
All rights reserved. Printed in the United States of America.
Published by Shepherd's Heart Music, Inc.,
3201 North 74th Street West, Muskogee, Oklahoma 74401

Shepherd's Heart

1-800-877-0406

www.dennisjernigan.com

ISBN 0-9765563-3-2

Edited by Israel Jernigan
Book Scan by Hannah Jernigan
Art design and layout by Israel Jernigan
Interior Photography by Hannah Jernigan
Back Cover Photo by Dani vanEttinger

Scriptural quotations in the devotionals not otherwise marked are from the New American Standard Bible (NASB) © 1973 by The Lockman Foundation. All other Scripture quotations not otherwise marked are from the Holy Bible, New International Version®. Copyright © 1973, 1978, 1984 by International Bible Society. Used by permission of Zondervan Bible Publishers. Other Scripture quoted from THE MESSAGE. Copyright © 1993, 1994, 1995, 1996. Used by permission of NavPress Publishing Group. Scripture quotations marked (NLT) are taken from the Holy Bible, New Living Translation, copyright © 1996. Used by permission of Tyndale House Publishers, Inc., Wheaton, Illinois 60189; (NKJV) are taken from The New King James Version © 1979, 1980, 1982, by Thomas Nelson, Inc. All rights reserved.

To *Melinda, Israel, Anne,
Hannah, Glory, Judah, Galen,
Raina, Asa,* and *Ezra*

I know God loves me because he made
you a part of my destiny in him.

⟶

To *Chuck* and *Jill Angel* and
the people of *New Community Church,*

Muskogee, Oklahoma,

Because you give my heart
a place to rest and be filled.

⟶

To *all* those who desire to know

who God says they are.

May the captive be set free, the lost be found, the
wounded be healed, and hearts be broken by God's
love. May lives be lived as sacrifices of praise and may
those lives be conduits of joy as they release the
precious aroma of intimacy with Christ to
those around them.

Contents

CONTENTS

Contents

Foreword

Since the emergence of the ministry of Dennis Jernigan, it has not been uncommon for those who have experienced it to draw a parallel between his music and that of another. Like the one before him, each carefully composed note bleeds with shameless honesty, intimate passion, empathetic soul, and boundless joy. It's the melody of the lonely, of the broken, of the redeemed, and the destined.

Hear him once and you quickly realize that his are more than songs-they are psalms. And, as one discovers in the life of King David, there is more to the psalmist than his music. There is reason before rhyme, molding before melody, and life before lyric.

As Dennis's, pastor and friend, it has been my privilege "to be there" for him and with him during times of healing, struggle, victory, and loss. I never tire of seeing the miracle of God birthing from these experiences the psalms that give release to the groanings of our spirit.

My thrill in commending this book to you is that I now get to share with others what has been one of my greatest blessings. For through these pages you now have the opportunity to be there and to share in the moment when the miracle happens. Hear what Dennis hears, feel what he feels when God breaks through with singing.

It is my promise that as you explore the pages that follow, you will laugh and cry, you will kneel with conviction and stand with inspiration as you discover more and more the destiny that God has for you!

Chuck Angel
Pastor
New Community Church
Muskogee, Oklahoma

Acknowledgment

I WOULD like to thank:

Father God for showing me more of who I am...my destiny.

Howard Publishing and Here to Him Music for yet another opportunity to share my heart.

John Howard, Gary Myers, Philis Boultinghouse, and Glenn Wagner for making me feel like part of the team...like family.

Trish Pfeifer and Robin Jamison for keeping the office running.

Robert and Peggy Jernigan for being a part of my destiny.

John Levens, John Hewitt, and Terry Skinner for being more than a band of musicians...for being my friends.

Kathy Law for giving so much, so freely to see my destiny come to pass. Paul Brothers for dreaming and challenging and for the joy of seeing life from the high places.

Matt Vandiver for being there.

Chuck Angel, Annie Herring, Keith Green, Jack Taylor, and Captain Kirk for being my heroes...and Chuck for also inspiring much of the music and ministry.

Before You Read On

LIFE IS A series of struggles. Sorrow. Difficult circumstances. Death. Relationships. Pain. Suffering. Sin. Most of us tend to grow thick layers of emotional skin that block the pain after a while. Our souls grow callous. I carne to a point in my life where I decided that I was tired of hiding my hurts and sin. I even talked myself into believing that my sin-homosexuality-was not sin at all but simply my identity-who I thought I was. All signs pointed to that "truth," so I gave in to it. The only draw, back to this acceptance was that I became more miserable than ever. What happened to change things?

In 1981, Jesus Christ intervened and set me free. The power of homosexuality was broken. My identity was forever changed in a moment. But the process of relearning who I really am has been an ongoing journey with the One who set me free.

Throughout this book, when I use the term homosexuality, you may put your own sin in the place of that word, because all sin is the same. It separates us from God. And in every case of sin, the remedy is the same. We all need a Savior; we need Jesus Christ. I have been told over the years, particularly by those who believe there is nothing wrong with homosexuality, that I am either brainwashed or that I was never homosexual. To those statements I say this: God's ways and thoughts are higher than mine. He calls homosexuality sin. Who is really brainwashed here? If I were never homosexual, I can think of better testimonies than homosexuality that I would find much easier to share-and more palatable to those I minister to (not to men, don more profitable).

My pastor recently shared about some of the scientific discoveries concerning the Shroud of Turin, an ancient burial cloth. Many believe it is the actual burial shroud of Jesus. Emblazoned on the cloth is the image of a man. That image was somehow burned into the cloth, much like a photograph is imprinted upon photographic paper. A burst of light causes photographic images to be captured on film. This appears to be the same process by which the image of the man was captured upon the Shroud of Turin. Could it be that the blazing light of God's resurrection power in the tomb of Jesus left such an image upon that cloth? Whether or not it is the actual image of Christ, the analogy still works: When Jesus transformed me from death to life with his resurrection power, his image and identity were emblazoned upon my heart. Dennis Jernigan as I knew him ceased to exist. Someone brand,new was raised up. God's Word tells me chat "if any man is in Christ, he is a new creature; the old things passed away; behold, new things have come" (2 Cor. 5:17).

For me, the struggle to know my identity began early in life. A boy who could play the piano was indeed an oddity in our small town. As a youngster, I was gifted by God with a deep emotional awareness of what was going on around me. Couple both these issues with the lies of the Enemy of God, and you find one confused little boy who grows up believing he is somehow different from other little boys, chat he was born to be homosexual. I do not believe we are born chat way. But we are all born sinners, and we all need a Savior. The truth is that I could not save myself. Because of a distant relationship with my earthly father, I honestly believed this was who I had been created to be. And the Enemy of God capitalized upon this belief.

From the day we are conceived, Satan fights to keep us from knowing God. We are all created in God's image, but because of our sinful state, we must be changed, born again. Satan knows this and goes out of his way to deceive us so chat we settle for far less than God's best in our lives. He is a liar and seeks to pervert anything and everything to keep us from knowing God. I know because I have been there!

Why a book on destiny?

Can we really know our destiny?

Can we miss our destiny? Have you ever wondered why you are where you are?

Are there habits, hidden sins, or weaknesses you wish you could deal with once and for all? Do you ever struggle with your identity, wondering who you really are? Find the answer to one of these questions, and you may just find the keys to unlock the doors to other unanswered mysteries of your life. I believe that my purpose, my destiny, my weaknesses, and my identity are all somehow interconnected in a deep way.

I personally believe that if we find our identity, we will find our destiny. And if we know our *identity* and our destiny, then we have powerful tools at our disposal for tearing down old habits (see 2 Cor. 10:3-5) and for shattering sin's hiding places in our hearts. If we know our identity and destiny, what was once a weakness can become a point of strength. I found my identity and destiny when Jesus found me and I entered into a holy relationship with him. Would you like to know who you really are and what God thinks of you? Would you like to discover your destiny, your reason for existence? Read on only if you dare...

Only if you dare realize how much more freedom you can know when you know Christ in an intimate way...

Only if you dare stop settling for second best in this life...

Only if you dare believe God might have a special plan and destiny for your life.

CHAPTER 1

We Are
STRONG
in the Lord

We Are Strong in the Lord

We wrestle not with flesh and blood
But with the forces of night,
We've overcome them by the blood
Of the King Lord Jesus Christ!

We are strong in the Lord in the strength of his might!
Strong in the Lord we will stand and fight!
Strong in the Lord as we stand and sing!
Strong in the Lord as we praise the King of kings,
Lord Jesus Christ!

Stand firm in the armor of our God,
And pierce the darkness with light.
All praise to the overcoming God;
Let us lift our sword and fight!

INSPIRATION

2 Corinthians 10:3–5
August 8, 1989

WHILE LEADING the body of Christ in praise, it became apparent to me that part of my job as a worship leader is to encourage those in the body to rise up and assume the identity God has given them. We are strong in the Lord-not by our own strength, but by his. We are called to be warriors who do not allow the Enemy to overrun us. We are called to storm the very gates of hell. This song came as an admonition to believers to walk in their true identities. It is a song of boisterous praise to our God, boldly proclaiming who we are as a result of who he is.

"I meditate on your precepts and consider your ways." *Psalm 119:15*

"BE STRONG IN THE LORD AND IN HIS MIGHTY POWER." —EPHESIANS 6:10

"God is faithful; he will not let you be tempted beyond what you can bear." —1 Corinthians 10:13

"If anyone is in Christ, he is a new creation; the old has gone, the new has come!" —2 Corinthians 5:17

4

Who Am I

I GREW UP A square peg being forced into a round hole! I was an emotional child with what is often perceived as a feminine gift inn our culture-playing the piano. Born into a farm family in a small rural community, I was confused by the many differing identity signals I received. Was I a sissy as the boys at school declared? Was I a selfish, prideful, arrogant little show-off concerning my musical abilities as I often felt (especially when every relative who visited was subjected to the repertoire of songs I had memorized-usually at the insistence of mother)? Was I ever going to be pleasing to my dad or to anyone else-or was I simply destined never to quite measure up? For the longest time, I felt my complete identity had been pre-determined by my surroundings, by other people, quirk of nature.

My dad and I were not close in an emotional sense. He worked a lot-both on our farm and at his regular job. According to my memories, our conversations always centered around one of two things: something he wanted me to do or something I had done wrong. My feeble perception became this: My dad does not love me; therefore, I am unlovable. Since I did not believe my father loved me, I tried to gain or earn his love and acceptance by the way I performed at school, on the basketball team, or at the piano. Subsequently, I perceived God in the same way. I was unlovable and in need of something to make me look better to my dad and to my

God. The only problem was that all of my perceptions were based upon lies!

So how did I begin to recognize the lies? First, I had to believe God's Word: There is an enemy who desires to destroy my life. Upon receiving this truth, .I had to realize that my dad and my God were not the enemy-the Enemy is the enemy! Satan tosses little half-truths and subtle lies into my thought stream. When I do not pull them out, they are carried into the depths of my thought processes, becoming a part of the pool of what I consider truth-and most often, a part of who I believe I am. I had to learn to recognize the lies, put them off, and then replace them with God's truth. It is in the truth, remember, that we are set free! When I pluck a lie out of my thought stream and cast it aside, I must then east the truth into the stream to replace it. When I replace the lie with the truth, my truest identity is allowed to surface. As the truth permeates the pool of my innermost being, I soon realize the joy of discovering who I am.

The desire to plunge deeper into the truth takes me to levels of freedom I could never have imagined!

I wrestle not with flesh and blood but with the real Enemy who desires to pervert my thoughts, my identity. He clouds the Light with darkness. But the truth is...

I have overcome me Enemy by the blood of Jesus Christ.
My identity forever changed when Jesus made me new.
With my old self forever buried, someone brand-new rises
up—still wrapped in old grave clothes, but free,
yearning for one more taste of freedom.

Like Lazarus, I am alive and somewhat mobile, but I desire to walk free of all the things that bind me from my past-from the death I formally walked in! The truth? My dad loved me and laid down his life for me. The truth? Jesus Christ did the same!

MEDITATION

- What are your struggles?
- If you had to describe who you are, what would you say?
- What does this mean in relation to your personal struggles?
- When are you your own worst enemy?

TRUTHS FOR MEDITATION

*"If anyone is in Christ, he is a new
creation; the old has gone, the new has come!"*
—2 Corinthians 5:17

*"Though we live in the world, we do not wage war as
the world does. The weapons we fight with are not
the weapons of the world. On the contrary, they
have divine power to demolish strongholds. We
demolish arguments and every pretension that sets
itself up against the knowledge of God, and we take
captive every thought to make
it obedient to Christ."*
—2 Corinthians 10:3–5

*"They overcame him by the blood of the Lamb and by
the word of their testimony; they did not love their
lives so much as to shrink from death."*
—Revelation 12:11

AS YOU GO TO SLEEP, ask the Lord to give you a vision of what
he sees when he thinks of you.

"Even in their sleep..."
—Psalm 127:2 NASB

Weapons of Warfare

WHEN JESUS FIRST set me free, the Enemy would often tempt me to slip back into my old way of thinking, my old sin patterns. Because Satan had dealt with me so much in the past, he knew which buttons to push. His efforts would wear me down, and I would feel weak and defeated. But I began to learn that God has provided me with weapons of warfare. I am not left alone to fight the forces of evil; God has equipped me for battle.

Satan used to sneak up behind me and say, "Go ahead. Watch that show or listen to that music or think that perverted thought." But God provided me with the weaponry of a new nature, and I learned to respond, "To watch that show or listen to that music or think that thought is contrary to my new nature. That is not who I am!" The process of learning about my new nature begins with learning about the nature of God, for it is his image that we reflect. When we learn who God is, we discover life-changing truths about ourselves.

A second weapon God has provided us with is relationship with Jesus. I love his written Word, but I do not have a relation-ship with a book! I have a relationship with the living Word of God— Jesus Christ! (see Rev. 19:13). We are not alone! He goes through the temptations and the trials and the tragedies with us!

Did you know that praise is also a weapon of warfare? When I need direction, I simply praise my God. I talk and sing to him, and then I wait and listen for his response to me. Praise be to God, not only has he provided us with spiritual weapons, but he has also provided us with spiritual armor. Ephesians 6 calls us to arms and instructs us to "put on the full armor of God, that [we] may be able to stand firm against the schemes of the devil" (v. 11). What is our spiritual armor?

First is the belt of truth. Several versions of the Bible say we are to "gird our loins with truth." In a physical sense, our loins are the source of life and serve as a picture of life and its sanctity. We stand firm in Christ, knowing that truth cannot be swayed.

Then we are to put on the breastplate of righteousness. With it, we cover our hearts-our core identities-with the truth that the blood of Christ cleansed us from all unrighteousness and left us covered with his righteousness. From the heart emanates our relationship to God (see Prov. 4:23).

And on our feet we are to wear the gospel of peace. Jesus Christ is the answer and hope for all the hopeless. Christ alone can bring peace to any storm in our lives and salvation from any bondage!

Upon our heads we place the helmet of salvation. In Christ, all is made new-even our minds. We keep our minds covered by the truth that we have been saved!

Finally, we take up the sword of the Spirit, which is the Word of God. God's Word is the truth. When Jesus was tempted (see Heb. 4:15), he overcame the lies of the Enemy by quoting the truth of God's Word!

When fitted with the armor of God, we will not be blindsided by the firey darts of the Enemy.

Past failures lose their power, for they have been dealt with.

Present thoughts will not overrun me, for I am in command of my thoughts and I make the final decision on what I believe.

The opinions of others do not bombard me, for I have decided to believe what God says about who I am—regardless of what I or anyone else thinks.

And now, when Satan attacks me and tries to wear me down so that I will give up, I do give up—but not to him.

I don't give up to the lies of the Enemy.
I don't give up to some thought or activity that is contrary to who I really am.

I don't give up to some fleeting feeling that clouds my view
of God for a momentary pleasure.
I give up to God.

One of the greatest battle tactics of all is this: When I am
weak, then he is strong.

To know Christ is to declare war on the Enemy. To war
against a spiritual foe, we must arm ourselves with spiritual weapons and put on the spiritual armor of God.

The psalmist says, "Let the high praises of God be in their
mouth, and a two-edged sword in their hand, to execute vengeance
on the nations [the enemies], and punishment on the peoples [the
demonic forces]; to bind their kings with chains, and their nobles
with fetters of iron; to execute on them the judgment written; this is
an honor for all His godly ones. Praise the Lord!" (Ps. 149:6-9).

This is part of your heritage—your destiny. Will you walk
in it?

MEDITATION

- What enemies in your life need to be overcome?
- What weapons have you neglected to utilize?
- How can praise to God be an effective weapon against the lies
  of the Enemy?
- In what are as have you given in to your feelings or to the
  Enemy? How can you take those areas back and give them
  up to God?

TRUTHS FOR MEDITATION

*"No temptation has seized you except what is common
to man. And God is faithful; he will not let you be
tempted beyond what you can bear. But when you
are tempted, he will also provide a way out so that
you can stand up under it."*
—1 Corinthians 10:13

*"We do not have a high priest who is unable to
sympathize with our weaknesses, but we have one
who has been tempted in every way, just as we are—
yet was without sin. Let us then approach the throne
of grace with confidence, so that we may receive
mercy and find grace to help us in our time of need."*
—Hebrews 4:15–16

Psalm 149 • Ephesians 6: 10–17

AS YOU SLEEP TONIGHT, ask the Lord to take back battle,
grounds in your mind that you have given up to the Enemy.

"Even in their sleep..."
—Psalm 127:2 NASB

CHAPTER 2

STAND up for Jesus

Stand Up For Jesus

Who you gonna call when the world grows dark?
Jesus is his name!
Who will be your Light anywhere you are?
Jesus is his name!
Who you gonna call with the pow'r to save you?
Jesus is his name!
Who defeated sin by the life he gave you?
Jesus is his name!
He is Rock and a mighty, mighty God
And a Warrior who will make a way!
He is a King and a Lion and a Lord
And a King arisen from the grave!

Stand up for Jesus and do not be afraid!
Stand up for Jesus and follow while he leads the way!
Stand up for Jesus, you soldiers of the Cross!
Stand up for Jesus! Our Savior is a mighty God!
Our King is an awesome God!

Who you gonna call when the battle rages?
Jesus is his name!
Who is a solid ground and the Rock of Ages?
Jesus is his name!
Who will be your peace when you're facing terror?
Jesus is his name!
Who will carry you, be your burden bearer?
Jesus is his name!

Stand up for Jesus and let us put the Enemy down!
Stand up for Jesus! We're taking back the stolen ground!
Stand up for Jesus! Praise him and stand in awe!
Stand up for Jesus! Our Savior is a mighty God!

Our King is an awesome God!
Stand up for Jesus! He's risen from the grave!
Stand up for Jesus and give the glory due his name!
Stand up for Jesus! Be who he says you are!
Stand up for Jesus! Our Savior is a mighty God!
Our King is an awesome God!

INSPIRATION

Romans 14:7-8
November 6, 1997

After a very hard month of numerous attacks from the Enemy, leaving me feeling like I wanted to die physically, I began to take the attacks the the Father and sing to him. When I get squeezed, who I really am comes out, along with the junk of the old me that still lies undetected and needs to come out! This song was a cleansing agent for my soul. As I declared who I am and whose I am, the old responses began to flow out and be replaced by the true responses of my born-again nature. Jesus stood up for me. I am a joint heir with Christ, inheriting his very strength to stand and accept the Cross. I can stand because he stood. I will stand up for Jesus.

"THE SPIRIT HIMSELF TESTIFIES WITH OUR SPIRIT THAT WE ARE GOD'S CHILDREN." —ROMANS 8:16

"You are no longer a slave, but a son: and since you are a son, God has made you also an heir."

—Galatians 4:7

"This is the message we have heard from him and declare to you: God is light; in him there is no darkness at all"

— 1 John 1:5

"I meditate on your precepts and consider your ways." Psalm 119:15

16

 # Started Editing Here... Couldn't take It any longer!

Between the Dark and the Light

AFTER GOD HEALED me of my shameful sin, I received this counsel from a close friend: "God has forgotten about your sin. So should you. There is no need to share my past with anyone."

While it is true that God had forgotten my sin, the Enemy still had a grip on my life because of this secrecy. I went into my marriage without telling my wife of my past. She knew I had dark secrets but felt it best to leave them alone. The Enemy had a field day with me in this regard. He constantly used this secret as an ace up his sleeve. His lies haunted me: *What if someone finds out about your past? You and your ministry will be ruined...and your wife will leave you.*

Though I knew God had healed, me, in despair I doubted that anyone else would accept me after discovering my past failures. I was so insecure in my identity that the Enemy was able to use even my own healing against me! As God would have it, though, in July of 1988, a friend reminded me of one of my favorite scriptures: "Oh give thanks to the Lord, for He is good; for His loving kindness is everlasting. Let the redeemed of the Lord say so, whom He has redeemed from the hand of the adversary" (Ps. 107:1-2).

Satan had kept me from freedom for five years by constantly threatening to shout my sin from the rooftop. God revealed to me that if I was truly redeemed, it didn't matter what I was redeemed from. His desire was to take my greatest failures and make them altars of hope for others, places where I could point and say, "Look where I have fallen and see what my God has done to restore me!" I decided to "say so," based purely upon the truth of my new identity. I am redeemed…a new creation!

Because I often share my testimony in public, my ministry has been picketed on several occasions by pro-homosexual groups. I have received mocking phone calls and letters because of my stance upon truth. During such dark times, I simply call upon the Lord to be the light I need. Because I brought my sin into the light, it is much easier to see his Light in me and to respond according to my true and new identity.

What is more difficult for me are the times of darkness brought about by other believers. The song "Stand Up for Jesus" was born after such a time. My heart was broken because a group of "Christians" circulated a letter falsely condemning me. All because of this letter, I was "uninvited" to minister at a gathering just two weeks before the event. The matter would not have been so painful if any of those who had circulated the letter had bothered to talk with me personally. I was blind-sided by those who profess light and was quickly reminded, the hard way, that the Enemy often disguises himself as an angel of light. As in the first case, the answer is still the same. I must call upon the Lord to be a light for me.

Dark times will come. Pain will come. Life's circumstances will often leave us caught between a rock and a hard place with seemingly no way of escape. What do we do during those times? We remember who we are and whose we are. We must call upon the Lord and keep standing for the Light no matter what. If he is Lord, then he can handle the darkness.

In darkness, the light is easier to see.
In pain,, the healing is easier to appreciate and enjoy.
In hopelessness, we gain a greater dependence upon the Lord.
In despair, our joy deepens as we realize his understanding and love.

MEDITATION

- Recall some dark times in your life.
- Who was the light, and what were the circumstances of the shining?
- In what ways does the Lord desire you to "*say so*" concerning your redemption?
- What darkness are you presently facing? How would you like to see the light of God's truth applied to this darkness?

TRUTHS FOR MEDITATION

"Give thanks to the Lord, for he is good; his love endures forever. Let the redeemed of the Lord say this—those he redeemed from the hand of the foe."
—Psalm 107:1–2

"This is the message we have heard from him and declare to you: God is light; in him there is no darkness at all. If we claim to have fellowship with him yet walk in the darkness, we lie and do not live by the truth. But if we walk in the light, as he is in the light, we have fellowship with one another, and the blood of Jesus, his Son, purifies us from all sin. If we claim to be without sin, we deceive ourselves and the truth is not in us. If we confess our sins, he is faithful and just and will forgive us our sins and purify us from all unrighteousness. If we claim we have not sinned, we make him out to be a liar and his word has no place in our lives."
—1 John 1:5–10

MEDITATE UPON THE DARK areas of your life as you fall asleep. Ask the Lord to shine his light into these areas so that you might wake up refreshed with the truth.

"Even in their sleep..."
—Psalm 127:2 NASB

Determining Factors

AFTER THE INCIDENT of being publicly attacked and falsely accused by so-called Christians, I went into a time of depression. For several months, I cried out to God but felt alone. Because I had already determined who I was and whose I was, I knew how I was to respond. I just didn't feel like it anymore. The hurt was too deep.

As the depression wore on, God was faithful to surround me with people who would not let me give up and to give me grace to carry on. I was encouraged when I was asked to sing on a project involving Max Lucado. I had dreamed of working with my brother Max because of my respect for him and looked forward to this opportunity. But it was not to be. Two weeks before Christmas of 1997, my sister-in-law's six-year-old nephew, Jordan, was tragically killed in a car accident. The funeral was scheduled on the same day as the recording project with Max Lucado. What would my Father have me do in such a situation? I felt he wanted me to minister to my family...and so I laid down my dream. Knowing my Father, I knew he knows best and always restores what the locust devours (see Joel 2:25).

Feeling the need for some time off, I loaded up my six oldest children and drove to Colorado for a week of skiing. I love to ski, and I especially love to ski with my children. But it was not to be. One by one, the children began to succumb to the flu! They spent the whole week in bed, and I felt like a lousy excuse for a father. How would God redeem this? Yet because I know what he is like, I had to believe he would.

Oh, there's more! Back home, as Christmas approached, I had decided to buy a go-cart for my children (I must admit I had always wanted one for myself). When we started the go-cart on Christmas morning, it ran for only a few minutes. The transmission was frozen up. The kids' gift was a huge disappointment to all of us. Once again, I felt like a failure as a father. Even though both instances—the ski trip and the go-cart—were beyond my control, the Enemy still used them as opportunities to come against my mind. Such instances seem trivial as I look back, but through the overabundance of trying circumstances, the Enemy got a foot in.

My point? Do I allow those circumstances to determine my identity? Do I allow them to lessen the truth or power of God in my life? Though life does bring pain and things do change, we have a constant God who remains with us, and we are his children.

Who I am and whose I am determine whom I follow, whom I serve, and whom I bow down to. When we know who we are in Christ, our holiness is determined by the holiness of Jesus: "It is no longer I who live, but Christ lives in me" (Gal. 2:20). A proper understanding of who I am and whose I am prepares me to face the sometimes harsh realities. I'm sad about the attack on my ministry, but I believe that Jesus wins in the end. And I keep on trusting God to give me the strength to persevere and see his destiny for me realized. I have been called to lead people to freedom. So I do that, regardless of what the Enemy might throw in my way. Of course, I respect and value the opinions and lives of others, but not to the extent that I compromise the integrity of Jesus Christ or his deter-mination of my value. And certainly not to the point where I stop fighting. Knowing Jesus is worth the fight!

Our status as new creations does not change though all falls apart around us.

God strengthened me through the attacks on my ministry. Little Jordan is with Jesus, and God does comfort. I went to ex-change the go-cart and asked God to show me what to do. Instead of exchanging it, I got my cash back. Then I drove down the road and felt prompted to pull into a lawn mower shop that sells go-carts, but it was closed. I went in, and the manager was there remodeling. He sold me a new cart with a guarantee to service the cart should any problems occur. God is Redeemer even of the little things...and I belong to him.

MEDITATION

- What types of circumstances get you down the most? Why?
- How do your circumstances affect your self-perception?
- How do your responses to those circumstances leave you feeling about yourself?
- How can God be Redeemer in death? How have you seen him redeem the small things of life?

TRUTHS FOR MEDITATION

*"I will repay you for the years the locusts have
eaten—the great locust and the young locust, the
other locusts and the locust swarm—my great army
that I sent among you."*
—Joel 2:25

*"I have been crucified with Christ and I no longer
live, but Christ lives in me. The life I live in the
body, I live by faith in the Son of God,
who loved me and gave himself for me."*
—Galatians 2:20

*"Christ redeemed us from the curse of the law by
becoming a curse for us, for it is written: 'Cursed is
everyone who is hung on a tree.'"*
—Galatians 3:13

*"Jesus Christ...gave himself for us to redeem us
from all wickedness and to purify for himself a people
that are his very own, eager to do what is good."*
—Titus 2:13–14

AS YOU PREPARE TO SLEEP, give the Lord freedom to bring truth where you feel most susceptible to wrong self-perceptions.

"Even in their sleep..."
—Psalm 127:2 NASB

From Victim to Victory

THE TRUTH sometimes hurts, but it always sets us free (see Joel 8: 32). Because we are used to being shamed by the Enemy and because our flesh doesn't particularly enjoy exposure to the light, we try to avoid honesty and transparency. If our identity is based on our performance, then hiding from the light is the natural response. Revealing a weakness or admitting a failure is tantamount to stamping *worthless* on our foreheads! Even when we fail, we feel we must hide our failures or cloud them over with excuses—or blame someone else.

Adam: "It was Eve's fault."

Eve: "It was the serpent."

Me: "That's just the way I am."

In each instance, we sacrifice a piece of our identity to the Enemy of God. To give up ground to the Enemy is to give up a part of our inheritance from our heavenly Father (see Rom. 8:1-17).

The battle for our minds is so very real. Think about it. As a man thinks in his heart, so he is (see Prov. 23:7). What we think about ourselves is the grid through which we view and live our lives. If Satan can pervert our way of seeing ourselves, he can capture ground that belongs to us—that belongs to God. When he captures one piece of ground, rest assured, he will hunt for more. What, then, are we to do? Because we know that the Enemy will attack and deceive, we can prepare for those battles. In fact, I believe that even after he has stolen ground, we should go on the offensive to take it back, for we have the power of Almighty God on our side!

When I realized I had been lied to concerning my sexual identity, I became ravenous in my hunger to know the truth. My attack was very simple: Identify the Enemy's position (his lies) and attack with the sword of the Spirit—the Word of God! If I am a new creation, then all the old is made new. What was homosexual before is heterosexual now. What I had felt was unlovable in me is now valuable and valid.

What I once saw as feminine (like my musical and emotional gifts), I now see as masculine and effective tools in the hands of the Lord.

Not only did this affect my thought process, it also affected my outward appearance. I allowed what was taking place on the inside to be demonstrated on the outside. My mannerisms began to change. My speech patterns and inflections began to change. The way I think about myself directly affects how I dress and where I go and what I see and hear and do!

Once I began taking back the ground that the Enemy had stolen, the snowball effect took place! I was now rolling over the Enemy instead of him rolling over me! Hallelujah! When the Enemy would tempt me to think or respond according to my past, I simply spoke the truth to him: That is not who I am any' more!

One thing I have learned from being a song receiver, or a song writer, is that no one decides for me what constitutes a "good" song. If God gives me a song, I—not the music industry—determine whether it is good or valid. In that way, I never have to worry about what others think of my music, and I am not bound by what others think. My identity as a new creation works much the same way.

My past failures do not determine my identity.
Present feelings do not determine my identity.
My parents do not determine my identity.
My job, skills, or talents do not determine my identity.
The lies of the Enemy do not determine my identity.
Who determines who I am? My heavenly Father!

If my Father says something about me, even if I cannot see it yet, I can rest assured it is so...and begin to put on that truth...and walk in it. I can no longer blame someone else for how I view myself. I cannot make the old excuse "that's just the way I am," because it is no longer "the way I am." I take back the stolen ground by simply being in relationship with my Father. His holy genes are now part of my inheritance from him. I must simply stand

MEDITATION

- What stolen ground in your life would you like to take back?
- What truths must you put on to take back that ground?
- What have you allowed to determine your identity?
- What do you think God thinks of you?

TRUTHS FOR MEDITATION

"The truth will set you free."
—John 8:32

*"The Spirit himself testifies with our spirit mat we are
God's children. Now if we are children, then we are
heirs—heirs of God and coheirs with Christ, if
indeed we share in his sufferings in order mat we
may also share in his glory."*
—Romans 8:16–17

*"Because you are sons, God sent the Spirit of his Son
into our hearts, the Spirit who calls out, 'Abba,
Father.' So you are no longer a slave, but a son; and
since you are a son, God has made you also an heir."*
—Galatians 4:6–7

*"Listen, my dear brothers: Has not God chosen those
who are poor in the eyes of the world to be rich in
faith and to inherit the kingdom he promised those
who love him?"*
—James 2:5

AS YOU PREPARE FOR SLEEP, ask the Lord to reveal to you anything you have allowed to determine your identity that does not lead you to the truth and to freedom.

"Even in their sleep..."
—Psalm 127:2 NASB

25

somebody big Big

CHAPTER 3

S OMEBODY

Big

Somebody Big

What is a mountain to someone
Who's strong enough to cast it into the deep blue sea?
What is a problem to someone
Who's strong enough to love somebody
Once lost as me?
I needed someone who was strong enough
To help my blind eyes see!
I needed someone who was strong enough
To rescue, set me free! Free!

Somebody big enough to part the biggest ocean!
Somebody big enough to calm the raging sea!
Somebody big enough to set my heart in motion!
Somebody big enough to save the life of me!
Somebody who can love me! Somebody who will care!
Somebody always strong enough and always there!
Somebody who can know me! Somebody I can know!
Somebody who can make a way where I can follow!
Somebody who is Lord of all and King of kings!
Somebody who could take my sin and set me free!
Somebody goes with me through and situation!
Somebody big enough is Jesus Christ, alive in me!

What could be hopeless to someone
Who holds the bery world within
His own mighty hand?
Nothing's impossible for someone
Who conquered sin, gave his life,
Now triumphantly stands!
I needed someone who would not turn back
When others turned from me!
I needed someone who could love like that—
Enough to die for me! For me!

INSPIRATION

2 Chronicles 20:6;
Matthew 19:26
June 25, 1997

ONCE AGAIN, I was unab le to be at the particular service in which my pastor, Chuck Angel, shared the teaching on the bigness of God...but I had already been meditating on the subject! As I flew to California for a ministry opportunity, I asked the Lord if he had anything for me. I got out my manuscript book and silently gazed out the window and let my heart go. At forty thousand feet it was not difficult to begin thinking about the magnitude of God's nature. What is difficult to comprehend is that his bigness dwells in my smallness! From Chuck's own life I had seen the bigness of God demonstrated as Chuck and Jill continually receive God's grace and wait on him in relation to their daughter Celeste and her need for God's healing touch. Is anything too big for God to overcome? Is any obstacle really an obstacle to God? Do we limit him because we choose to see from our own perspective rather than his? I know I do.

"WHAT IS IMPOSSIBLE WITH MEN IS POSSIBLE WITH GOD." —LUKE 18:27

"I meditate on your precepts and consider your ways." Psalm 119:15

"Who is this? He commands even the winds and the water, and they obey him." —Luke 8:25

"In his great mercy he has given us new birth into a living hope through the resurrection of Jesus Christ from the dead." —1 Peter 1:3

How Big is God?

SOMETIMES LIFE SEEMS like a never-ending ocean with a series of storms. A peaceful moment may appear every so often, but by and large, the ocean of life is one stormy place! A few years ago, I felt God calling me away from a church staff position I had held for eight years. Leaving this position meant leaving the security and shelter I had known and moving my family and ministry to me middle of nowhere! Hearing God's voice was so very difficult at times. I asked him specifically to speak through my parents about what I should do. Not that I wanted them to make the decision for me, I simply wanted God to make his will very clear to me. Asking him to make himself known through my parents seemed logical. When my dad said he felt it was time that I share music on a full-time scale, I was at peace because I knew God had really spoken to me. Once I knew I have heard God, it becomes easy to take that step "out of the nest" and follow his leading. Speaking to my heart, Jesus says "peace, be still" to my storms of uncertainty.

Just how big is God to me?

He is bigger than my sin.

He is bigger than any problem I may face.

He is bigger than any pain, sorrow, or suffering this life may bring.

He is big enough to be the source of my very exis tence.

31

What is God like to me? That can best be illustrated through the many examples of his faithfulness to me, like when I needed to clear my conscience of all the hurt I had caused others. When God set me free of my sin, he began to woo me toward greater wholeness by showing me that every person I had sinned with, I had also sinned against. Even though I was free, I still wore those pesky grave clothes that kept me from walking around in my freedom!

I was still bound if I could not face those I had wounded. I was not free if the Enemy still held me captive to "what if others find out." I was still captive if my thoughts toward God were hindered by guilt and shame.

To be released, I needed to seek forgiveness from those I had wounded. This seemed to me like an impassable ocean. I would need someone to part those waters of fear and doubt for me...and my God fit the bill! As I was obedient to make a list of those from whom I needed forgiveness, he was faithful to bring about holy coincidences. After suddenly meeting someone face to face whose name was on that list, God gave me the grace to humble myself and seek that person's forgiveness. And the ocean was parted—and a greater measure of freedom came into my life as a result of God being bigger than my fears.

There have been times in my life when I have not been able to see a way out of terrible circumstances, when I have been wounded because I risked loving and trusting another, when I have so sinned against God I did not see how he could possibly love me.

Does my lack of sight mean God is not at work?
    No. Not seeing a way out means I must learn to
      rest in his presence and wait on his answer.
Does being wounded mean I stop risking to love or
    trust another?
    No. Being wounded is like fire that burns our
      hearts' impurities, revealing our deep need for
      Jesus.
Does my sin keep God from loving me?
    No. My sin is yet another opportunity to expe-
      rience the power of God's love and forgiveness
      through my own repentance.

How big is God? He is bigger than my circumstances. Bigger than my wounds. Bigger than my sin. There is nothing he can, not handle!

MEDITATION

- How big is God to you?
- What circumstances can you not see a way out of?
- When have you been wounded in such a way that you feared loving or trusting others?
- When have you sinned against God but were ashamed to seek his forgiveness?

TRUTHS FOR MEDITATION

"One day Jesus said to his disciples, 'Let's go over to the other side of the lake,' So they got into a boat and set out, As they sailed, he fell asleep. A squall came down on the lake, so that the boat was being swamped, and they were in great danger. The disciples went and woke him, saying, 'Master, Master, we're going to drown!' He got up and rebuked the wind and the raging waters; the storm subsided, and all was calm. 'Where is your faith?' he asked his disciples. In fear and amazement they asked one another, 'Who is this? He commands even the winds and the water, and they obey him.'"
—Luke 8:22–25

"What is impossible with men is possible with God."
—Luke 18:27

"Do not be afraid. Stand firm and you will see the deliverance the Lord will bring you today.... The Lord will fight for you; you need only to be still."
—Exodus 14:13–14

WHILE YOU SLEEP, allow the Lord to show you specific ways he desires to demonstrate his greatness, or bigness, to you.

"Even in their sleep..."
—Psalm 127:2 NASB

Hope for the Hopeless

I CAME TO THE point of desperation in 1981. I had trusted another with my deepest hurts and failures in the hope that he could help me. After I had laid my heart out, this person took what I had shared and used it to exploit me physically. When the one I had placed my hope in violated me in this way, I gave up. I was a worthless, defeated excuse for a man. I even tried to end my own life. But as I contemplated the peace death would bring, I became terrified when I realized I did not know what eternity might hold for me. All my life I had longed for acceptance and love and had placed my hope for that acceptance in man. But I was soon to learn that true hope comes from one source alone: Jesus Christ.

What is hope? Hope is wishing for something with expectation of its fulfillment. When I was a young boy, I remember knowing I had a major problem with sin, specifically as it related to my identity and sexuality. Even then, I had the knowledge that I needed God, and I begged him to change me, I wished he would change me. But my expectations always ran aground upon the reality of my own failure. With each failure, I grew more and more bound, and hope seemed farther and farther away.

What is hope? Hope is having confidence and trust. Since I had become enslaved to what I thought others thought of me and my performance, I became a needy child and grew into a needy adult. I wanted to be loved and accepted so much that I would put my hope in anything or anyone I felt might fulfill those desires. As I put my confidence in others, not God. Gifts and performance cannot earn

Think this is what he meant 34

love and acceptance from God or bring personal fulfillment. I remember times of trusting individuals and then being used by those individuals. My trust shattered, I soon felt there was no one I could trust at all. Not even God. It became apparent that there was no hope for me.

What is hope? Hope is knowing the source of or the reason for hope. When people feel hopeless, they tend to fall into despair. When they fall into despair, they are filled with a sense of futility and defeat.

What is hope?

Hope is finally realizing that I have been loved and accepted all along.

Hope is understanding that I can know God in an intimate and personal way on a moment-by-moment basis.

Hope is knowing that Jesus Christ is the only true source of understanding my purpose and identity.

Hope is accepting that anything apart from his truth is not truth! Truth sets us free; it does not lead us into more bondage!

Hope is being able to be honest with others and knowing they can be trusted.

Hope is trusting God when others betray and use me.

Hope is knowing Jesus himself was betrayed and used.

Hope is believing that I am fully accepted and loved by the God who gave me life in the first place.

Hope is putting off the old lies and putting on the truth of my new identity in Christ.

Hope is the realization that knowing Jesus Christ is worth everything.

Hope is knowing I am known by God Almighty and that I am his child...completely and irrevocably!

Hope is Jesus Christ in me.

MEDITATION

- Have you ever been betrayed by someone you trusted?
- How has this affected your life?
- In whom or what do you place your hope?
- What is more important—the acceptance of men or the approval of God?

TRUTHS FOR MEDITATION

*"Though he slay me, yet will I hope in him; I will
surely defend my ways to his face. Indeed,
this will turn out for my deliverance, for no godless man
would dare come before him!"*
—Job 13:15–16

*"God has chosen to make known among the Gentiles
the glorious riches of this mystery, which is Christ in
you, the hope of glory."*
—Colossians 1:27

*"We have put our hope in the living God, who is the
Savior of all men, and especially of those
who believe."*
—1 Timothy 4:10

*"He saved us, not because of righteous things we had
done, but because of his mercy. He saved us through
the washing of rebirth and renewal by the Holy
Spirit I whom he poured out on us generously through
Jesus Christ our Savior, so that, having been justified
by his grace, we might be come heirs having the hope
of eternal life."*
—Titus 3:5–7

*"Because God wanted to make the unchanging nature of
his purpose very clear to the heirs of what was promised,*

he confirmed it with an oath. God did this so that, by two unchangeable things in which it is impossible for God to lie, we who have fled to take hold of the hope offered to us may be greatly encouraged. We have this hope as an anchor for the soul, firm and secure."
—Hebrews 6: 17–19

1 Peter 1 :3–9

PREPARE FOR SLEEP by asking the Lord to show you any people or things in which you have placed your hope. Give him me freedom to lead you to place your hope and confidence where it truly belongs—in a living and loving relationship with him.

"Even in their sleep..."
—Psalm 127:2 NASB

CHAPTER 4

you will
be my
ROCK

You Will Be My Rock

When stormy weather comes against me, ravaging my heart...
Some storms seem so long they never cease.
When stormy weather comes against me, take my where you are,
In your arms a constant state of peace!

You will be my Shelter! A place where I can run!
A Rock! A sure Foundation that cannot be overcome!
You will be my Refuge! A place where I can go!
A Rock that will surround my when the winds begin to blow!

When the winds blow and the waves crash all around me,
You are like and island in the middle of the sea!
When the winds blow, stormy waves about to drown me,
You will come surrounding with a Refuge of Peace!

You will be my Fortress! A place where I can hide!
A strong and mighty Warrior who will never leave my side!
You will be my Father! My heart will be your home!
A Rock that can't be shaken when the winds begin to blow!
You will be my Rock!
You will be my Shelter!
You will be my Rock!
You will be the Shelter for my soul!

When everything around me seems to fall into the sea,
Crushed by waves that beat incessantly,
When everything I've trusted in just falls away from me,
In your arms I find security.

INSPIRATION

2 Samuel 22:2–3;
1 Corinthians 10:1–13
July 3, 1997

This song came in several stages but was first inspired by a sermon by Chuck titled "The Rock." I initially began receiving it as a personal word from the Lord as I heard him singing the words from his point of view in my life: "I will be your Shelter...a Place where you can run...a Rock, a sure Foundation that cannot be overcome..." But as usual, the Lord allowed me to see that the adversities of my own life were actually meant as tools for pouring out his life through me to others. One night my son Judah Paul came into our bedroom during a thunderstorm. As I assured Judah of God's presence and protection, another portion of the song was born for him. Later on in the month, I had the opportunity and blessing of meeting one of my favorite singers, Morris Chapman. I was excited to meet him and humbled to hear him say that he and his wife had been greatly ministered to by my music. As we talked, God began to show me how to pray for Morris and his family, and the rest of the song was born. I would encourage you to sing this over others from God's point of view as you teach the song, because it really is the truth!

41

"I meditate on your precepts and consider your ways." *Psalm 119:15*

"THE NAME OF THE LORD IS A STRONG TOWER; THE RIGHTEOUS RUN TO IT AND ARE SAFE." —PROVERBS 18:10

"You are my Father, my God, the Rock my Savior"
—Psalm 89:26

"The Lord is with me like a mighty warrior."
—Jeremiah 10:11

Peace in the Storm

As I WRITE THESE WORDS, a storm has just passed over our farm. In the midst of the tempest, it seemed as if the world would fall apart. Lightning illuminated the darkness every few seconds, threatening to invade our peace. Wind made attempts at tearing the shingles from the roof. Thunder shook the house and rattled the windows. Rain pelted the rooftop with intermittent patterns of random rhythms. These elements bombarded every inch of the outer shell of our home, and the noise and uncertainty led my son to the edge of my bed. Fearful and needing comfort, my son's heart just needed to hear his dad's voice telling him, "It's going to be all right, son. I'm here with you." At those words, my boy quietly made a bed on the couch near our bedroom door. Being close to his father brought peace enough that the little boy was asleep almost as soon as he lay down his head.

Do we sometimes respond to the storms of life like little children? I know I often do. It would be one thing for my son to be out there and exposed to the elements of the storm and quite another for him to be confined to the safety of his father's house. Why did my son fear? Because he had been scared by the tornado reports—reports of death and destruction and loss of possessions. At the first sounds of rain, wind, or thunder, he remembered those reports and was ready to believe that a twister was closing in on our home.

The Enemy gives us false reports about the storms of life. He tells us that we cannot weather the storms, that we are alone and without hope. Listening to his lies leaves us operating in a false reality. We begin to feel abandoned, alone, afraid, and unsure. We are weakened by a lack of truth. Listening to the false reports of the Enemy leaves us unprotected and exposed to the whims of the storms, when all along we do have a Shelter—a Shelter that promises to cover us like a warm, dry house built upon a sturdy, unshakable foundation. Reality is what God calls reality. The reality of the storm hurts, but it does not leave us without hope as the Enemy would have us believe.

My heart has been ravaged by the storms of life because I believed Satan's reports. I was crushed like a rudderless boat that got tossed upon the rocks by every wave that came along. I had no anchor without faith and trust in Christ. A man in a boat with no anchor tries to grasp anything he can hold on to. Anything looks good when hope is nowhere in sight!

The things I used to put my trust in during the storms now make me sick as I see how futile and pathetic they are from Christ's view. When I felt less than a man, I put my hope in the affections of men. My hopes were dashed every time I was used, and my heart was smashed upon the rocks of their abandonment. When I struggled to be accepted for my talents, I anchored my heart to my talent. My heart was crushed by the waves of humiliation I felt when this anchor gave way, and there were always others more talented than I. I put my hope in my ability to "fake" my way through life. I could put on a good show outwardly while dying inwardly.

Because I trusted Satan's false reports, all that mattered was what people thought of me. The weight of guilt and shame of my hidden life left me shipwrecked in mind and adrift in spirit. After I was set free from homosexuality, I needed direction, and I found it easier to trust other men who appeared more spiritually stable than I. I abandoned my will and blindly and mindlessly submitted to the will of "godly" authority only to find myself crushed upon the rocks of the selfish whims of men, which left me once again feeling used and worthless. I needed an anchor. I needed a sure foundation for life. I needed a Rock.

When Jesus rescued me, I found peace in the storms of life. The truth of his reality was a strong, sure foundation that enabled me to withstand the storm. He was there in the stormy nights of my emotional healing, telling me, "It's going to be all right, son. I'm here with you." Just like my truthful words of reassurance calmed my son's fears, so too Christ's words of assurance calmed mine, and I found peace. Truth always brings peace if it is received.

Being close to my Father brought peace enough that this little boy could finally rest from the constant berating of the storms of sin and the winds of the Enemy's lies. I learned that calling out to my Father and listening for his voice would bring peace, because knowing he is going through the storms with me gives me peace. Knowing he is a shelter around me makes the storms appear as they really are-outward influences at best that cannot possibly harm the inward peace of my identity or the inward intimacy of my relationship with him. Storms will assail and rail against the outside of my house, but on the inside there is safety and peace because the truth is-my house is strong and is built upon a sure foundation—a Rock— Jesus Christ.

MEDITATION

- What storms have you faced in your life?
- What do you do when the storms seem unending?
- What false reports about the storms has Satan whispered in your ear?
- What truthful words of assurance does Christ have for you?

TRUTHS FOR MEDITATION

"Therefore everyone who hears these words of mine and puts them into practice is like a wise man who built his house on the rock. The rain came down, the streams rose, and me winds blew and beat against that house; yet it did not fall, because it had its foundation on the rock. But everyone who hears these words of mine and does not put them into practice is like a foolish man who built his house on sand. The rain came down, the streams rose,

*and the winds blew and beat against that
house, and it fell with a great crash."*
—Matthew 7:24-27

*"Peace I leave with you; my peace I give you. I do not
give to you as the world gives. Do not let your hearts
be troubled and do not be afraid."*
—John 14:27

GIVE THE HOLY SPIRIT the freedom to expose Satan's false reports about the stormy areas of your life where you do not fully trust him. Then as him to show you the shelter of his presence as it applies to these areas.

"Even in their sleep..."
—Psalm 127:2 NASB

Knowing Him

K<small>NOWING</small> G<small>OD</small> is life. Knowing him intimately makes the harsh realities of life bearable and able to be overcome. Knowing him makes life worth living, even when we have to face stormy times or fiery trials. Knowing God is knowing abundant life now, not at some future and distant place we call heaven. Don't get me wrong; I look forward to heaven. But my life and eternity are now! How do I face the death of a friend and still experience joy? How do I face the opposition of the Enemy yet still enjoy every step of the journey? I am able to live this life with joy and hope because I *know* God.

One way we get to know God better is by learning about his names. We associate names with certain characteristics. When I think of my son Israel, I think of someone who is a hard worker, a joyful soul, and a challenge on the basketball court. When I think of my daughter Anne, I think of maturity beyond her years, patience and kindness to animals, and desire to please me. With the Lord, it is no different. To know his names and what he calls himself reveals to us what he is like...and how we can trust him to respond to us.

God's Word tells us that the name of the Lord is a *Strong Tower* (see Prov. 18:10) where the righteous, those who have been made new creations in Christ, can run and be safe. The character of God is like a tower, a fortified place of shelter from me Enemy—a refuge.

When the storms of temptation have come against me, I have learned to reach for the *Rock*—the name for Jesus—and cling to him (see 1 Cor. 10:4). The winds of doubt and waves of lies will bombard my soul. When those times come, I have learned what my God calls himself a Rock (see Ps. 89:26).

I see God as my personal Refuge when I feel assailed (Ps. 46: 1). I crawl upon this firm foundation and hide there in the truth of his inner being until the storm passes over. In this way, I enjoy the benefits of peace even before peace has actually come to the physical realm.

Truth is what God calls truth, and he tells me he can calm the seas of life!

There is a time to stand boldly against the Enemy...and then there is a time to hide myself away from the onslaught, especially right after intense times of spiritual battle or victory...when I am most susceptible because I am being spiritually poured out. During those times, he is called *Fortress* (see Ps. 18:2). The fiery darts and arrows of the Enemy's lies fall powerless when I am hidden in the presence of my Fortress. In Christ, in that hidden place reserved for me, my truest core identity cannot be touched!

Over and over the Word describes God as our loving *Father*. That the creator of the universe is also my Father is too overwhelming to think about for very long! I want my heart to be a place where he is welcome at all times. His heart is my home and my rightful place of dwelling as his child. Because of God's great sacrifice to make me his own, it is quite obvious that he is also a protective Father. If my children were being attacked and overcome by someone trying to harm or violate them in some way, do you think I would stand idly by and just watch? No way! I would defend my family and home with every bit of my strength! I am an earthly father and I feel that way, so how much more would our heavenly Father?

In fact, he is so intent upon seeing his children safe that he does not wait for the attacks to come. He goes on the offensive as a jealous Warrior and removes all threats to our safety (see Jer. 20: 11). And God has called us to rule over the powers of darkness as he does. The only way we can do that is by battling against that darkness like he does...by taking up the fight in wisdom and in truth.

In calling God by name I become intimate with him. In calling out to him and to each particular trait of his holy character, I learn to trust him...and to call out to him quickly.

MEDITATION

- Have you ever run to God as a Strong Tower? How did he protect you?
- Why is the idea of God as Rock comforting?
- When have you used God as a Refuge, a hiding place?
- What is a fortress? How is God a Fortress?
- How is he like your Father, protecting his children?
- How is he like a Mighty Warrior fighting on your behalf?

TRUTHS FOR MEDITATION

For you died, and your life is now hidden with Christ in God."
—Colossians 3:3

"He will call out to me, 'You are my Father, my
God, the Rock my Savior.'"
—Psalm 89:26

"I love you, O Lord, my strength. The Lord is my
rock, my fortress and my deliverer; my God is my
rock, in whom I take refuge. He is my shield and the
horn or my salvation, my stronghold. I call to the
Lord, who is worthy of praise, and I am saved
from my enemies."
—Psalm 18:1-3

WHAT IS YOUR FAVORITE aspect of being hidden in Christ? Dwell on this peaceful "place" as you sleep.

"Even in their sleep..."
—Psalm 127:2 NASB

make me more free

CHAPTER 5

make me
MORE
free

Make Me More Free

Make me more free! Free me!
More free from my old life!
More free in my new!
Make me more free! Free me!
More free in loving you!

With wings like and eagle,
My heart made to fly
Over sin, over sorrow
To new realms of life!
From glory to glory,
My gaze fixed so high
That I only see Jesus,
The love of my life.
Make me more free! Free me!
With pow'r over sinning,
More power to love!
Make me more free! Free me!
Fill me with your pow'r to love!

Help me to see! Free me!
To see you and know you,
To know I am known!
Help me to see you see me
And know I am yours alone!

INSPIRATION

Psalm 40:1–3; Galatians 5:1
June 1, 1996

For several weeks, my pastor had been teaching us from the book of Colossians, basically leading us into greater depths of grace and freedom in Christ. From my perspective, his sermons were love-filled challenges to put off the old and rise up and walk in our new and true identities as the sons and daughters of Almighty God. On this particular Saturday evening (at this time we met in the YMCA on Saturdays because another church used it on Sundays), I began to receive this song as soon as pastor Chuck began speaking. I had received the entire song as you now hear it by the time he had concluded his teaching! Since that time, God has used it as a personal inspiration for me to continue to walk in my truest identity in him. May you be as inspired to do the same—to walk in the grace and truth of who you really are.

"LET US…APPROACH THE THRONE OF GRACE WITH CONFIDENCE, SO THAT WE MAY RECEIVE MERCY AND FIND GRACE TO HELP US IN OUR TIME OF NEED."
—HEBREWS 4:16

"You have made known to me the paths of life; you will fill me with joy in your presence." —Acts 2:28

"Those who hope in the Lord will renew their strength. They will soar on wings like eagles, they will run and not grow weary, they will walk and not be faint."
— Isaiah 40:31

"I meditate on your precepts and consider your ways." Psalm 119:15

Getting My Wings

THE BOY HAD BEEN raised by creatures of the darkness. Yet he was not one of them.

These evil creatures lived in a cave beneath the surface of the earth and only ventured beyond their self-imposed prison in order to capture others and indoctrinate them, enslaving them to their dark way of life.

The boy had actually come from a race of winged men, those who were born to fly. But the creatures of darkness had bound his wings, and they were dismissed as useless appendages that had lost their usefulness through the evolutionary process. He soon learned it was better not to mention the wings—to deny their very existence. The dark ways seemed right to him, and his life seemed "normal." It was all he knew. So what if he tripped and fell a lot? So did everyone else. So what if he was constantly bombarded by injuries and the limits of the dark life? So was everyone else.

His painful, dark life continued until the day he caught a glimpse of fluttering whiteness streaking by the cave entrance. Captivated and curious, he approached the surface and was again surprised by the brilliant whiteness and graceful motion of *wings*! Wings just like the ones on his own back...wings that were no longer useful...wings that were a part of his long- forgotten identity. In a daze over what he had seen, he was astonished and blinded as one of the winged men snatched him from the pit and began bathing him with pure light.

Wanting to fight at first, his fears melted into peace as the winged men surrounding him began to unbind the clothing of darkness that bound his wings.

He knew that he was somehow seeing himself in their faces, yet he could not move until he accepted the truth: He had believed a lie about himself. He had been born to fly yet had given years to the darkness and its misery, thinking that was all he deserved. As he embraced his true identity, his wings began to move...and the boy ascended above the darkness and took his rightful place among the winged men!

Isn't that a true picture of our lives in sin? Even after we are saved, we often gravel in the darkness of the past since that is all we have known, since that is who we believed we really were. Yes, perhaps I was once homosexual, but that was not God's intention for me. When he redeemed me, he gave me a brand-new identity (see 2 Cor. 5:17). Having a brand-new identity after living my "old" life for so long was quite revolutionary. I had believed that I was born homosexual, yet God said my homosexuality was part of my old nature and that he had given me a new nature! That meant I had to put off a lot of what I formerly believed to be true and, in turn, put on what he now revealed to me to be true! Yes, just as I had to learn a whole new way of thinking about who God is, I also had to do the same in regard to my own character, or nature.

I also had to face the truth that I could not have two natures. There is only one "me." The old me is dead and buried with Christ. The new me is learning—much as a child learns to crawl, walk, then run—how to live my new life! If God is all he says he is, and if I am his child, then certain things are part of my heritage—they are my birthright, my identity as being "of God"—and I must cling to the truth of who I really am! Failure or sin on my part does not constitute a rejection of that identity. It simply reaffirms my great need to be in close relationship with my Father. After all, the gifts and calls of God are irrevocable! You are who he says you are no matter what you feel or perceive! (see Rom. 11:28-36).

We really have only touched the tip of the iceberg of who God is. But what does that mean for us? We have only touched the tip of the iceberg of who we are! I find it easier and easier to put off the old me because I like who God is showing me I am!

Do not give up in your quest to know him. As a warrior, he has fought and won the war, and he will lead you through your personal battles. He will give you your wings!

MEDITATION

- Where would you be without Jesus Christ?
- Luke7:47 tells us that those who understand that they have been forgiven much, love much! How much do you love him?
- What does it mean to be his *child*, his *possession*, a *new creation*, a *royal subject*, a *priest*, a *warrior*, *accepted*, *beloved*, his *servant*, his *delight*?

TRUTHS FOR MEDITATION

"You have made known to me paths of life; you will fill me with joy in your presence."
—Acts 2:28

"We proclaim to you what we have seen and heard, so that you also may have fellowship with us. And our fellowship is with the Father and with his Son, Jesus Christ."
—1 John 1:3

ASK THE HOLY SPIRIT to show you your spiritual wings. As you sleep, spread your wings of faith and discover more of your true identity in Christ.

"Even in their sleep..."
—Psalm 127:2 NASB

Make Me More Free

WHAT IS freedom? Is freedom the opportunity to do anything you want as long as it feels right? No.

Freedom means *not being imprisoned or enslaved*. Jesus set me free from sin and the bondage of my old identity. I thought I was free when I could do as my body and soul dictated. This type of "freedom," the freedom to sin, only led me to death and destruction. True freedom always results in life. Always.

Freedom means being *at liberty*. At one time I was controlled by the Enemy to a certain extent. He knew how to get me to think wrong thoughts. I was controlled by my feelings rather than by God's feelings for me. Jesus set me free to submit willfully to his control of my life. This type of free submission always leads to life. Always.

Freedom means *to be governed by consent*. I was not set free to become a mindless zombie for the Lord. The beauty of the freedom we find in Christ is that we have the choice to follow him. Submission to love and holiness can by no means be compared to the bondage of sin. I submit to Christ and to my new identity because he loves me dearly. I can follow a love that lays down its life for me.

Freedom means *not controlled by obligation or the will of another*. Jesus offered me salvation and a brand-new identity as a free gift. I did not have to earn it. All I had to do was receive it. I willfully follow him because of the love and faithfulness he has demonstrated to me.

Freedom means *not being affected or restricted by a given condition or circumstance*. The things that used to affect my behavior and restrict my ability to function rationally—bitterness, lust, disappointments, and emotional wounds—no longer affect me as they once did. I have seen them for what they are—powerless!

Freedom means *not being subject to external restraint*. No outward circumstance—even prison—can affect my inward identity.

Nothing. Why? Because I am free! How free do we have to be to be considered free? When a mighty oak tree bears fruit and a seed is produced, new life begins for a brand-new oak tree. Everything that oak will ever be is already inside that seed. You could truthfully hold up an acorn and say, "Look at this mighty oak!" No, the tree is not actually grown yet, but with each phase of growth, the tree becomes more of what it already is. We, as new creations, are no different. You could look at a baby in Christ and say, "Look at this mighty man of God!" That new creation is every bit a child of God as the believer who has known Christ for fifty years! With each phase of growth, the new creation becomes more of what he or she already is. Identity cannot change once we are in Christ; levels of maturity and understanding can.

When I was first set free, I was as much a new creation as I would ever be. Why did I still struggle with sin? Because I had been ingrained for twenty-two years with the notion that I was homosexual, yet in an instant that identity was changed. I was like a baby learning to crawl and then stand and then walk and then run...and then soar above the old me! I was alive yet bound up in all the lies and misconceptions about myself and God. I wanted more than just to be alive. I wanted to use that aliveness, that freedom, to spread my spiritual wings and soar above sin and sorrow and the cares of this world. I wanted life, and I wanted it abundantly.

By putting off the old and putting on the new, I spread my wings of faith and soared above sin and sorrow to discover new vistas of reality I never dreamed possible.

I am no longer bound to sin or its power.
   I have power over sin!
I no longer fear the risk of rejection love brings.
   I willfully lay down my life...like Jesus.
I no longer wonder about why I exist.
   I know beyond a shadow of a doubt because I know
      the One who gave me life.

I know my Creator in an intimate and freeing way! He has made me to soar with wings of faith. Like an eagle soars over the rocky crags and treacherous cliffs, I now set my eyes on Jesus and spread my wings. I am learning to ride the winds of the Spirit and soar above the temptations of life. Trials and tribulations now represent opportunities to experience God's grace, and each encounter with my God leaves me amazed that life just seems to keep getting better and better!

This is freedom. To know God and to be known by him sets me free. I only want more! Make me more free, Father. I love you!

MEDITATION

- What does freedom mean to the world?
- What does freedom mean to you?
- What are some areas in which you would like to experience more freedom?
- What does freedom have to do with identity?

TRUTHS FOR MEDITATION

"Do you not know? Have you not heard? The Lord is the everlasting God, the Creator of the ends of the earth. He will not grow tired or weary, and his understanding no one can fathom. He gives strength to the weary and increases me power of the weak. Even youths grow tired and weary, and young men stumble and fall; but those who hope in the Lord will renew their strength. They will soar on wings like eagles; they will run and not grow weary, they will walk and not be faint."
—Isaiah 40:28-31

ASK THE LORD to allow you to sleep and dream of all the things you want to soar above in this life. See it as the truth...and let this truth set you free.

"Even in their sleep..."
—Psalm 127:2 NASB

CHAPTER 6

All I
USED
to be

All I Used To Be

I saw no way to ever rise again.
Deep in my heart each time I looked within,
Indelible the shameful stain of sin
That used to grip my heart with all I'd been.
Then one day you came raining,
Washing over me,
Washed away sin proclaiming,
"This child is redeemed!"

All I used to be you washed away
When you redeemed me!
All I used to be erased away.
Completely you cleaned me!
Pouring through my heart like a rainy day!
Wiping every single sin away!
Washing, changing me completely!
All I used to be was bound in sin!
The bondage restrained me!
All I used to be made whole again,
My Lord, when you claimed me!
Pouring through my heart like a rainy day!
Wiping every single sin away!
Washing, leaving me completely changed!

I never thought that I would ever see
The day that I could walk completely free.
And then a cleansing rain fell over me,
Releasing all I'd ever hoped to be!
That's the day you came raining,
Washing my heart clean!
Washed away sin proclaiming,
"This child is redeemed!"

INSPIRATION

*2 Samuel 13–18;
John 14:27*
July 18, 1997

IN NOVEMBER 1996, my pastor, Chuck, received a word from the Lord that as a church we were to come into 1997 expecting God to display his character in our midst. The Lord has also begun stirring a series of messages in Chuck's heart for the following summer. Each teaching would bear the title of a popular movie to remind us of a spiritual truth. Just before the summer of 1997 began, God gave me a vision of receiving a song for each sermon as a way of reinforcing what he was speaking to us through Chuck. Since I travel more in the summer, I was not able to be there, but I did the next best thing. Each week I called Chuck, and asked him to share his heart with me so that I might meditate with him on what God was doing. "All I Used to Be" came as I meditated on the fact that the blood of Jesus had completely erased all my sin and had given me a brand-new identity!

"IN ALL YOU WAYS ACKNOWLEDGE HIM, AND HE WILL MAKE YOUR PATHS STRAIGHT." —PROVERBS 3:6

"Put on the new self, created to be like God in tr righteousness and holiness." —Ephesians 4:24

"He who began a good work in you will carry it on to completion until the day of Christ Jesus." — Philippians 1:6

"I meditate on your precepts and consider your ways." Psalm 119:15

Back to the Basics

I LOVE BASKETBALL, and I love to play the game. You might even call me a basketball player. But is my skill such that I could play in the NBA? Hardly. The skills required to play the game and the skills required to play in the NBA are on totally different levels. Knowing God and walking in freedom are also on different levels. Our freedom can only rise to the NBA level as we *practice* being who he says we are.

One young basketball player neared the point of rage with himself he once again missed what would have been the game-winning free throw. He hated the feeling of failure—the feeling knowing he had disappointed his teammates, let his coach down, and snatched defeat right out of the jaws of life! This young man overflowed with natural talent and had been endowed with a sixth sense for basketball. To look at him you would think, This kid is unstoppable. He can write his own ticket.

He knew all the right things to do. Hadn't the coach told him and told him time after time? "Take a deep breath. Rest the ball in the palm of your right hand. Guide the ball with your left hand. Let the ball roll from your fingertips and follow completely through in one fluid motion." Yet he continued to fall back into his old playing habits.

Sensing his son's frustration and not wanting him to give up, the young man's father took him aside as the dejected home crowd slowly filed out of the gymnasium. "Son, I know you know this: You have been blessed with an amazing talent. But until you follow your coach's instruction, you will never realize your fullest potential—you will never be what you have been gifted to be."

The boy's heart had been broken. "Dad, what can I do? I really want to change. I just don't know how."

The crowd was all gone now. The boy and his father were left standing at the free-throw line. "Son, explain to me the proper technique of shooting a free shot." The boy spoke all the right words and even pantomimed the technique for his dad. "Now, son, pick up the ball and show me the proper form for shooting a free shot." The boy threw the ball—and missed!

"Don't you see, son? You *say* all the right things, but you don't *do* all the right things. Until you can put off your bad habits and put on the good ones, you'll be just another basketball 'wannabe.' Is that what you really 'wannabe'?"

From that night on, me boy diligently practiced his technique...in front of his coach...in front of his dad...even in front of the bathroom mirror! Soon, the old habits became so distant in his memory and the new habits brought such success that it was as if he had never struggled to shoot a free throw in his life. He was soon given another opportunity to win a game at the free-throw line. And the ball went in! There would be other times as well. Some he won. Some he didn't. But in putting off the old and putting on the new, he was never again haunted by failure...because failing only reminded him to go back to the basics and rest in what he knew was right.

True freedom will only bloom in your life when you put on the truth of who God says you are. *Knowing* who God wants you to be is not the same as *practicing* who he wants you to be. When life gets complicated and failures abound, turn your heart and mind back to the basics. Remember who you are in Christ, practice being who God says you are, and in time, you'll be walking in the NBA hall of freedom.

MEDITATION

- What of the old you was washed away?
- What can you do to help the maturing/growth process of your identity along?
- Are there any old habits you need to take off?

- What truths do you need to put on in their place?
- Do you feel truly free in Christ?

TRUTHS FOR MEDITATION

"Clothe yourselves with the Lord Jesus Christ, and do not think about how to gratify the desires of the sinful nature."
—*Romans 13:14*

"For the perishable must clothe itself with the imperishable, and the mortal with immortality. When the perishable has been clothed with the imperishable, and the mortal with immortality, then the saying that is written will come true: 'Death has been swallowed up in victory.' 'Where, O death, is your victory? Where, O death, is your sting?' The sting of death is sin, and the power of sin is the law. But thanks be to God! He gives us the victory through our Lord Jesus Christ. Therefore, my dear brothers, stand firm. Let nothing move you. Always give yourselves fully to the work of the Lord, because you know that your labor in the Lord is not in vain."
—*1 Corinthians 15:53–58*

"You, however, did not come to know Christ that way. Surely you heard of him and were taught in him in accordance with the truth that is in Jesus. You were taught, with regard to your former way of life, to put off your old self, which is being corrupted by its deceitful desires; to be made new in the attitude of your minds and to put on the new self, created to be like God in true righteousness and holiness."
—*Ephesians 4:20–24*

ALLOW THE LORD to show you areas where you have not taken off the old. Then receive the new and put it on in the place of the old.

"*Even in their sleep...*"

—Psalm 127:2 NASB

The Road to Freedom

PEOPLE ASK ME so often, "Was your healing instantaneous or was it gradual?" My answer to both questions? "Yes!"

I can honestly say that the power of perversion was instantly broken in my life because I suddenly had the power to rise above the most appealing of temptations. I now find it difficult to believe I was ever involved in any such perversion. I have been given a new nature—I am a new man!

Growing Up, I often heard preachers speak about human-kind having two natures. I always wondered what that really meant. Are there two Dennis Jernigans who make up who I am? That idea didn't make sense to me, but because I accepted what people told me rather than searching out truth for myself, the Enemy had me right where he wanted me—*confused*. Now I see that if I have an old nature *and* a new nature, then I am not really healed. I believe a better description of being born again is that there is a dead Dennis and a living Dennis. The old Dennis has no more power. He's dead. The power belongs to the living. Since I believed right away that I was somebody brand- new, by faith I began to immediately see myself from God's perspective, placing his thoughts and proclamations about me above my own! Instantly!

But healing is also a process. I had lived twenty-two years believing one way about God and about myself. I told myself early in my journey that I was willing to walk out this process of freedom for another twenty-two years—or more—if that was what was required. Overcoming homosexuality was the easy part. Getting to the root of my self-destructive thought life was a different matter. Unless we kill the root of the weed of sin in our life, that weed will always sprout back up. God has taken me on a trip through the garden of my life, pulling up all sorts of weeds...and he continues to do so.

God's Word says that "the fear of the Lord is the beginning of knowledge" (Prov. 1:7). I fear (or honor) God by putting aside what I once thought or believed and putting on what his Word tells me to be true. After all, his ways and his thoughts are higher than mine. He is God. I am not!

The journey of healing is much like the description of Jesus raising Lazarus from the dead. As soon as Lazarus was raised, he was living and free, but he was still bound by his grave clothes. To be raised from the dead is, in itself, quite an awesome thing; not being able to enjoy your life once you are raised up would be a shame. But as soon as the grave clothes were removed from him, he was truly free!

What were some of my grave clothes? Certain relationships. I had to cut off those who enabled me to sin. Certain music. For more than ten years I refused to listen to any music, secular or sacred, that led my mind away from truth. Certain mannerisms and attitudes. I decided that if God had brought about a change in my heart, then that change should logically be visible on the outside. Certain places, attitudes, and mementos from my past. I exchanged these for something better: God's best.

I now have years of freedom under my belt, but I still get up every day and realize that I cannot make it one step without God's love and power in my life. Apart from his grace, I would surely fall away. Does that statement mean I am any less whole? No way! Just dependent upon God's strength and not my own!

The journey toward Jesus, toward wholeness and freedom, is never-ending. When I fall or trip or make a wrong turn, I get up or steady myself or turn around and keep heading toward Jesus. The joy is knowing he will meet us at each place and will be faithful to complete the work he has begun in our hearts!

MEDITATION

- Is freedom a one-time occurrence or an ongoing journey?
- How has redemption changed your outlook upon life?
- How does this affect the level of hope you have?
- How does this affect the visions and dreams of your life?

TRUTHS FOR MEDITATION

"The fear of the Lord is the beginning of knowledge,
but fools despise wisdom and discipline."
—Proverbs 1: 7

"If a kingdom is divided against itself, that kingdom
cannot stand. If a house is divided against itself, that
house cannot stand."
—Mark 3:24–25

"He who began a good work in you will carry it on to
completion until the day of Christ Jesus."
—Philippians 1:6

Proverbs 3 • John 11:1-46

ASK THE HOLY SPIRIT to give you insight as to where you are
on the journey of life.

"Even in their sleep..."
—Psalm 127:2 NASB

Alive and Growing

My IDENTITY IS NOT determined by me, by my past experiences, by my present feelings, or by any circumstance of life. My identity is determined by the One who gave me birth.

Just as a person's physical appearance is determined by the genes of his or her parents, so my spiritual "look" or identity is determined by the genes of my spiritual parent! Just as I cannot be anything less than the son of my physical parents, so I can, not be anything less than the son of my heavenly Father once I have been born again.

When I was born again, I was made a child of Father. Even though I may not have a full understanding of all I am, I am no less than a child of God. When an acorn drops from an oak tree, everything that an oak tree is, is contained in that seed. It doesn't matter what level of maturity that seed may have at the moment. It is no less an oak tree than if it were 150 feet tall!

Being a child of God is no different. Just because I am a baby in my relationship with the Lord does not make me any less a new creation than if I were a fully mature adult. As a seedling is just as much an oak tree as it will ever be, so a brand-new believer is every bit as much a complete child of God as the mature believer.

Maturity and identity are two different things. My identity is unchangeable—it is who I am. Maturity is simply becoming more of who I already am!

Growing in and maintaining an intimate relationship with Father is the key to knowing who I am. And praising God has been an avenue of intimacy in my relationship with him. I praise him by acknowledging who he is and how he benefits my life. I tell him everything! As I have grown in my praise of him, I have been dumbfounded and amazed to discover that my God praises me! How can that be? How does the Almighty Creator God praise the ones he created by his might?

He praises us as a parent would praise a child.

God praises us as a parent would praise a child for coming to a deeper place of maturity.

The Enemy wants to persuade us that we are hopeless failures.

God praises us through his delight in us simply because we are his.

The Enemy wants us to feel we must perform for God's acceptance and approval.

God praises us by saving, "Well done, my good and faithful child."

The Enemy would have us believe we are worthless.

God's praise of us builds us up in the center of our true identity.

The Enemy directs us to flounder around like a ship aimlessly adrift on the sea.

When children fall and get hurt and dirty, do parents send them away to bind up their own wounds or clean up their own filth? No. Good parents take their children into their laps, cleanse away the dirt, and bind up their wounds. If I, as a parent, want to do this for my child, how much more does our heavenly Father want to bind up our wounds and cleanse our sin? How much more does our heavenly Father desire that we walk in ever greater levels of maturity and understanding of our own identity as his children?

I can no longer excuse sin by saving, "That's just the way I am." Why? Because I have been given a brand-new identity, and it is time to put into action the reality of who I am. It is time to let my heart grow and mature in the life with which I have been infused.

Like me mighty oak that grows from the small acorn, like the child who is no longer satisfied to simply crawl, I want to be all he has made me to be!

MEDITATION

- What are some of the "That's just the way I am" statements you have believed about yourself?
- What does God say about you in these areas?
- What will it take for you to see yourself as God sees you?
- If you were God, how would you encourage or praise you as a child?

TRUTHS FOR MEDITATION

"Jesus declared, 'I tell you the truth, no one can see the kingdom of God unless he is born again.'"
—John 3:3

"Provide for those who grieve in Zion—to bestow on them a crown of beauty instead of ashes, the oil of gladness instead of mourning, and a garment of praise instead of a spirit of despair. They will be called oaks of righteousness, a planting of the Lord for the display of his splendor."
—Isaiah 61:3

Psalm 1:3

ASK THE HOLY SPIRIT to let you hear Father praise you as you sleep tonight. Don't be afraid to know the truth about the good things Father thinks of when he sees you!

"Even in their sleep..."
—Psalm 127:2 NASB

CHAPTER 7

You are
MY
God

You Are My God

Worldly wisdom could not save me
From my sin or from the grace!
But you came shining,
You unblinding me!
You came redeeming me!
From my past you set me free
And opened up my eyes to see
That you come raining life,
Sustaining life
To set your people free!

You are my God! You are my Lord!
You are my King! You are God!
You will reign forever!
Reigning in glory and power!
Reigning in glory and power and life!
You are my God! You are my Lord!
You are my King! You are God!
You will reign forever!
Reigning in glory and power!
Reigning in glory and power and life!
Forevermore!

One day all will boy the knee
To One who reigns eternally!
Princes, paupers, sons, and daughters...
All we call humanity!
Every tongue will too confess
That Jesus reigns in righteousness!
Almighty God and Lord of all!
My Lord! My God! My Righteousness!

You are Savior! You are Redeemer!
You are King and you are Lord!
Father, Spirit, Christ my Redeemer!
Reign in me forevermore!

INSPIRATION

Proverbs 3:7;
1 Corinthians 1:18–21
December 27, 1996

THE INSPIRATION for this song came after a hectic Christmas. To be honest, I had not enjoyed the season. Because of all the hype and commercialism, I had almost missed Jesus. This song was one of those God just dropped on me in the midst of my frustration. It is my declaration that I was glad the holidays were over so I could get on with my life!

"IF ANYONE WOULD COME AFTER ME, HE MUST DENY HIMSELF AND TAKE UP HIS CROSS AND FOLLOW ME."
—MARK 8:34

"God chose the foolish things of the world to shame th wise; God chose the weak things of the world to shan the strong."

—1 Corinthians 1:27

"Consider it pure joy, my brothers, whenever you face trials of many kinds, because you know that the testing of your faith develops perseverance." —James 1:2

"I meditate on your precepts and consider your ways." Psalm 119:15

Worldly Wisdom

WORLDLY WISDOM says to "do whatever feels right to you." For a period in my life, I succumbed to that philosophy. Why do I say "succumbed"? The word *succumb* means "to submit to an overpowering force or yield to an overwhelming desire; to give up or give in." I came to a point where I could not explain my thoughts or behaviors to myself. When the Enemy saw my vulnerability, he swooped in for the kill. He sent men who had already given in to their lusts and perversions with and explanation for my thoughts and feeling. Their reasoning was that much more believable because they seemed to read me like a book. For a brief period, I experienced a measure of peace because I had at least settled on who I was. I told myself: *This is who I am. This is who I will be.*

I was walking in worldly wisdom, and much of the turmoil ceased...but for only a season. Because worldly wisdom is merely a counterfeit, a mockery of what is good and right and pure and true, I soon became so miserable that I almost gave away my mind completely. I came close to wholeheartedly believing that Satan's ways are better than God's. Believing that what is right is wrong and what is wrong is right is called "reprobation." It nearly happened to me.

When God intervened in my life and showed me truth, I lunged for that truth. I felt as if I were on the edge of a cliff and that if I did not hold on to him, I would surely fall away into utter destruction and damnation. While following worldly philosophies and beliefs, I had experienced death rather than life. I was ready for life, and I leapt for the chance to know it!

My past has become a part of my present ministry. If I had been allowed to choose a testimony, I would not have chosen mine. No matter how much me world openly embraces the sin of homosexuality, it still leaves a sense of shame and disgust in the minds of most people, and I do not find particular pride in revealing it! As I have shared my testimony, I have heard some interesting conversations and comments from those who have chosen not to follow Christ but have chosen to fulfill the lusts of their flesh. I have been told, "A person cannot overcome homosexuality." "Once gay. Always gay." "You could never have been that way." "You are a liar." Yet my life speaks something different.

The world tried to tell me who I was, and for a while I believed it. But when it came to making a choice, I chose life. and I chose godly wisdom. God's Word says, "See to it that no one takes you captive through philosophy and empty deception, according to the tradition of men, according to the elementary principles of the world, rather than according to Christ" (Col. 2:8). To know Christ is to know and experience life. To embrace the teachings of worldly wisdom is to embrace death. The moment I cut off the wisdom of me world, I immediately began to experience hope and joy and me acceptance and the embrace of God himself!

God has called us to walk in an ever-deepening realm of maturity—still sons and daughters but not immature babies who are "tossed here and mere by waves, and carried about by every wind of doctrine, by the trickery of men, by craftiness in deceitful scheming" (Eph. 4:14).

Whom will you believe—the world or the God who created that world? Whom will you follow—the deceiver or the one who leads to redemption and life? Would you be free? Then there really is only one choice. His name is Jesus.

He will not leave you alone in your struggle for freedom. He is a jealous and protective God who walks through the healing process with his children. Be wise. Know Christ.

MEDITATION

- What does the wisdom of me world tell you about yourself?
- Is change possible, or should you just accept who you "really" are?
- Where does worldly wisdom break down?
- How does God reveal the truth to you and open up your blind eyes to see?

TRUTHS FOR MEDITATION

"Then we will no longer be infants, tossed back and forth by the waves, and blown here and there by every wind of teaching and by the cunning and craftiness of men in their deceitful scheming."
—Ephesians 4: 14

"See to it that no one takes you captive through hollow and deceptive philosophy, which depends on human tradition and the basic principles of this world rather than on Christ."
—Colossians 2:8

WOULD YOU ALLOW the Lord to reveal worldly wisdom to you as you sleep tonight? Trust him to lead you to greater depths of his wisdom.

"Even in their sleep..."
—Psalm 127:2 NASB

Who is Your God

GODS COME in many forms, and I am sad to say that I have I worshiped at the feet of several. In part, the dictionary defines a god as "the principal object of faith and worship." I now believe there is only one true God. Yet there have been times when I held other gods as the principal object of my faith and worship.

There was a time when I put my faith in my own strength and worshiped my *accomplishments*. I thought that since no one else cared about me, I had to care about myself and make my own destiny. I thought people would like me when they heard me play the piano or when they heard me sing. But I could not have a relationship with my gifts, and death was the result. There was always someone who could play or sing much better than I could. My god was not as powerful as I thought.

At other times I have put all my faith and hope in some *possession*. Have you ever hoped for something that would lift you above your weaknesses? I have. As a young boy, I wanted a pair of shoes called PF FLYERS. The ads said that by wearing PF FLYERS, I would "run faster and jump higher!" But once I got my PF FLYERS, I was still the same. Nothing had changed! I was crushed. My faith and hope could not be realized because it was wrongly placed.

Have you ever looked forward to some event as being your hope for peace, only to have that event happen and feel as empty as ever? As my college graduation approached, many influences upon my life were converging at once. I was in a stormy relationship with Melinda; I was contemplating suicide; I was struggling daily with perverse sexual thoughts and with my sexual identity; I was about to step into the future and had no idea what that future would hold. In my mind, graduation would be like a big shove into some new understanding of what life means. I eagerly looked forward to it. That big day came and went so quickly. The reality that nothing had changed for me hit me like a ton of bricks. Melinda was going on to a better life without me. I had failed at suicide. My thought life was more overwhelming than ever. I was convinced I had been born homosexual. And then I realized a harsh fact: All the peace and security I had enjoyed in my friends during the past four years was about to change forever...and I fell apart.

I remember several times when certain *people* have been the principal object of my faith and worship. Needing affirmation is not a bad thing, but where we go to have that need fulfilled can be the difference between life and death. I find myself drawn to people who make me feel good about myself. Again, that is a natural thing; but how I respond to that affirmation is vital. My life used to look like a merry-go-round. Someone affirms me; I cast all my hope and expectations upon them. They let me down; I am crushed. I need more affirmation; I drive them away and hit the bottom. Someone else affirms me; I throw all my attention to them. No real relationship. No real life. Only a cycle of death...because the object of my faith and worship was nothing more than flesh and blood—and often as needy, or more so, than I.

It was only when I placed my faith and worship in the one true God that this cycle began to break. You see, I found out quickly that God will not let me down. He does not leave me, and he does not forsake me. I found that he is big enough to handle all my frailties and bigger than any problem or weakness I might have. He is willing to walk through my healing as he actually facilitates that healing in a back and forth, deeply intimate and loving relationship—with me.

Jehovah God is the only god deserving of my faith and worship. He is embodied as Father, Holy Spirit, and Jesus Christ the Son. He is not some distant, ethereal, nebulous being; he is an ever-present, all-powerful, all-good, well-defined person! And that person happens to love me. We are in relationship. True relationship produces life as a natural by-product.

He is my God.

My Lord.

My Friend.

My Companion.

The object of my faith whom I worship with my life...
because my God radically transformed my life by his
power.

How can I not worship him?

I remove all else from the throne of my life and allow him alone to occupy that place. That throne? My heart and mind...my life.

MEDITATION

- What are the gods in your life?
- How do you give the Lord his rightful place in your life?
- How do you know you are serving the right god? Clue: Does life or death result?
- Where does the power to do what is right come from?

TRUTHS FOR MEDITATION

"You shall have no other gods before me."
—Exodus 20:3

"Whoever sacrifices to any god other than the Lord must be destroyed."
—Exodus 22:20

"They exchanged the truth of God for a lie, and worshiped and served created things rather than the Creator—who is forever praised. Amen."
—Romans 1:25

"Therefore, my dear friends, flee from idolatry."
—1 Corinthians 10:14

*"Then he called the crowd to him along with his disci-
ples and said: 'If anyone would come after me, he
must deny himself and take up his cross and follow
me. For whoever wants to save his life will lose it,
but whoever loses his life for me and for the gospel
will save it. What good is it for a man to gain the
whole world, yet forfeit his soul? Or what can a man
give in exchange for his soul? If anyone is ashamed of
me and my words in this adulterous and sinful
generation, the Son of Man will be ashamed of him
when he comes in his Father's glory with
the holy angels.'"*
—Mark 8:34–38

WOULD YOU LIKE to know life rather than death? Allow me
Lord to reveal other gods you worship. As you sleep, give him the
throne of your mind.

"Even in their sleep..."
—Psalm 127:2 NASB

85

Hands in My Pockets

THE WORLD is confused. I used to be confused. Confusion feels like being on an ocean of conflicting ideas, thoughts, or doctrines. Every wave represents another possible belief or "what if" or "if only," offering no concrete handle. God's Word is clear in this matter: "The one who doubts is like the surf of the sea driven and tossed by the wind. For let not that man expect that he will receive anything from the Lord, being a double-minded man, unstable in all his ways" (James 1:6-8).

I used to be that unstable man. One day I would believe God loved me. But the next time I doubted him, my mind was consumed with perverse thoughts about myself. One day I would think people liked me and accepted me. But the next time they let me down, I was devastated and felt unlovable. One day I would think I could be healed of all my sin. But the next time I fell, I was convinced it would never happen. I was aimless and unreliable. Like a Ping-Pong ball that hits a ceiling fan, I bounced around the world never sure of where I would land...or if I would land.

As a small boy, I would look at other boys and see their speech patterns and mannerisms and realize I did not do the things they did or talk the way they did. I did not carry myself as a little boy should. I am still reminded of those inadequacies when I see men or boys with their hands in their pockets. As a child, I would never do as the other boys did; I never put my hands in my pockets whenever we were standing around. I felt I did not measure up to them and was, therefore, somehow unworthy of walking around like the other boys. I thought that to do so would only highlight how different I really was because I would somehow look less masculine than the other boys. My remedy? Just don't put my hands in my pockets, and I'll be okay. Sad, huh?

But don't most of us experience inadequacies? Maybe they aren't as bizarre as mine were, but they're feelings of inadequacy or not measuring up nevertheless. I have heard women say things like, "If only I had her looks, life would be so much easier." I have heard men say things like, "If only I had been born into money like he was, I could conquer the world."

Inadequacies are a part of life. They are part of what weaves us together as believers, but they are also part of what makes us susceptible to the lies of the Enemy. Think about it. Sin leaves an emptiness in our hearts. Jesus fills the void. Yet we still hunger and thirst for more affirmation and love because we are still so aware of our weaknesses.

The Enemy knows this and throws our weaknesses in our faces because he knows we will seek to cover the feebleness caused by our insecurities. Once those insecurities come, we are hit with yet another wave of doubt that tosses our minds into chaos. What do we do?

I decided a long time ago that I would have an anchor for my soul, a place to latch my heart that would hold fast through any weather and be able to withstand any wave's force. I decided mat God's truth is true for me...not what others say or do...not what I feel...not even what I see. There has to be a standard, a place to anchor our souls. And for me that standard, that anchoring place, is Jesus Christ. What this means is that even when other obstacles are thrown into my path, I will choose to see and believe what God calls true, no matter what. This is not always easy because the Enemy hates solid ground and works to destroy those who seek it...and those who stand upon it. That is why I can "count it all joy" when I encounter various trials, because I know the testing of my faith—the attacks of me Enemy—means that I am on the right track. It means that my faith will produce endurance, and that endurance ensures I am complete in my identity, lacking nothing. When the Enemy attacks, I ask God for wisdom and guidance. I don't jump to conclusions. We are all in the same boat—princes, paupers; rich, poor; young, old; man, woman.

We all need an anchor.
We all need a Savior.
We all need Jesus.

How do I stand now when I gather with other men? I stand, with my hands in my pockets. This is my reminder to myself, my declaration to myself, that I am a man: whole, complete, and lacking in nothing!

MEDITATION

- What is your mind anchored to?
- How can you place your trust in Jesus and be anchored in those doubting times?
- What are some of the "what ifs" or "if onlys" of your life?
- What do you need to do to replace them with something more concrete?

TRUTHS FOR MEDITATION

"For though we live in the world, we do not wage war as the world does. The weapons we fight with are not the weapons of the world. On the contrary, they have divine power to demolish strongholds. We demolish arguments and every pretension that sets itself up against the knowledge of God, and we take captive every thought to make it obedient to Christ. And we will be ready to punish every act of disobedience, once your obedience is complete."
—2 Corinthians 10:3–6

"Consider it pure joy, my brothers, whenever you face trials of many kinds, because you know that the testing of your faith develops perseverance. Perseverance must finish its work so that you may be mature and complete, not lacking anything. If any of you lacks wisdom, he should ask God, who gives generously to all without finding fault, and it will be given to him. But when he asks, he must believe and not doubt, because he who doubts is like a wave of the sea, blown and tossed by the wind. That man should not think he will receive anything from the Lord; he

is a double-minded man, unstable in all he does."
—James 1:2–8

AS YOU SLEEP, ask the Lord to reveal places in your life where you are not anchored. Then ask him to show you how to cling to him in these areas.

"Even in their sleep..."
—Psalm 127:2 NASB

CHAPTER 8

With
MY
Praise

With My Praise

My soul trusts in thee
When my thoughts
Are surrounded by the Enemy.
My soul trusts in thee,
And with my heart
I surrender, Lord, to thee.

And with my praise
I trust in thee!
And with my praise
You scatter the Enemy!
And with my praise
I lift my soul to thee!
And with my heart
I surrender, Lord, to thee!
I surrender, Lord, to thee!

I would never make it one day
Without your love in my life!
You're my Rock
When the world sweeps over me!
Lord, so many times
I don't see a way
So just keep holding me tight,
For I know
That I need you desperately!

INSPIRATION

Psalm 149:5–9
March 11, 1987 and
November 10, 1997

THIS SONG was born as I was in the middle of learning to express my heart in honesty and transparency to the Lord. When the Enemy would lie to me, I discovered that his attack meant God was trying to create something through me. So I began to sing my prayer to Father and put down the lies. This song was born as a result. The second verse came in the midst of dealing with direct and very personal attacks upon my character and ministry. I would not make it one day without the Rock of Jesus to stand upon. this song is a testimony of God's sustaining power in my life as I seek an intimate relationship with him through worship and praise.

"I WILL PROCLAIM THE NAME OF THE LORD. OH, PRAISE THE GREATNESS OF OUR GOD!"

—DEUTERONOMY 32:3

"He is your praise; he is your God, who performed for you those great and awesome wonders you saw with your own eyes."

—Deuteronomy 10:21

"The Lord is my strength and my song; he has become my salvation. He is my God, and I will praise him, my father's God, and I will exalt him." — Exodus 15:2

"I meditate on your precepts and consider your ways." Psalm 119:15

With My Praise

I GREW UP in the church, yet I really never knew what it meant to actually worship God—even though I was in the music ministry! What that tells me is that we often go through me motions of relating to God without really knowing him at all. For many, worshiping God is simply a ritual that has no meaning. People can sing or lift their hands or dance in worship until they are blue in the face and never knew God intimately. fact, we can become so focused on what we do and so pleased with our own performance that we totally disregard the one we intended to acknowledge—the Lord! I was one of those people for so long.

In 1981, I moved in with a friend in Oklahoma City. This friend loved Jesus and had an intimate flowing relationship with him, and this intrigued me. I wanted to know Jesus in the same way. I was tired of the performance and ritual I had come to know as worship, as church. As my friend slowly and sensitively exposed me to the truth of God's Word and love, my heart began to yearn for an outward expression of what was taking place on the inside of me. With every bit of ground I regained from the Enemy, I experienced a deeper level of intimacy with Father.

My college degree was in church music, and I found it difficult to find a job when I got to Oklahoma City. But God provided—sort of. Driving a school bus, though not what I had envisioned for myself, was exactly what God desired for me because it set me up for some very intimate encounters with him. For several hours each day between my morning and afternoon routes, I would sit at the piano. Since I did not know how to have relationship with God, I decided I would follow the example of those who I knew did! Many times I simply sang right through the Psalms, because I knew that David was a man after God's own heart even though he had committed grave offenses toward him. As I sang King David's words, I began to experience great freedom in my soul. The words were acting as cleansing agents for my mind. They brought peace to my emotions helped me see more clearly. They helped me change my mind about who God was...and who he wanted me to be! As I went on, my friend and I would meet in the garage of another friend and seek God in prayer and worship around an old upright piano. Even though I only knew a few little worship choruses, sang them to Jesus with all our hearts. This was where I first I learned some of the secrets of worship-of truly knowing God in an intimate way—that have been a source of strength and fulfillment to me that truly exceeds my wildest dreams.

What does praising and worshiping God have to do with knowing my destiny or walking free from sin? Praise is simply expressing gratitude to God for what he does for me and in me. Worship is expressing to Father my deepest feelings toward him—and then allowing him to speak or sing truth back to me. Worship is relationship. Praise is a component of worship that helps me take my thoughts captive by filling my mind with the truth.

God is good.
  Thank you for your goodness!
God is mighty.
  Thank you for your strength!
God is faithful.
  Thank you for not giving up on me!
God is Redeemer.
  Thank you for changing me.

Praise puts down the Enemy, for at the name of Jesus, demons have to flee. Praise is a weapon I can use to put the Enemy in his place—beneath my feet! Praise helps me put off the lies and replace them with the truth. Praise frees my soul to commune with God in intimacy!

God frees me. I thank him. He is blessed, and I am changed. My feelings of gratitude lead naturally into a back and forth, giving and receiving connection of intimacy no human relationship can come close to.

With my praise, I know truth.
With my praise, I know freedom.
With my praise, I connect with God.
With my praise, I overcome the Enemy.
With my praise, I know God...and he knows me.
Bless you, Lord!

MEDITATION

- What is your soul?
- How can each of these elements—mind, will, emotions—trust in the Lord?
- How do you surrender these elements to the Lord?
- What do you do when the Enemy assails your thoughts? When your emotions are overwhelming you? When you desire to sin but know that is not who you are?

TRUTHS FOR MEDITATION

"Let the saints rejoice in this honor and sing for joy on their beds. May the praise of God be in their mouths and a double-edged sword in their hands, to inflict vengeance on the nations and punishment on the peoples, to bind their kings with fetters, their nobles with shackles of iron, to carry out the sentence written against them. This is the glory of all his saints. Praise the Lord."
—Psalm 149:5–9

ASK THE LORD to help you freely praise him even in your sleep. In this way, your mind will be a little more renewed when you awake!

"Even in their sleep..."

—Psalm 127:2 NASB

I Would Never Make it One Day

WHEN SIN HELD ME captive and God set me free, my first response was deep, intense, emotional weeping. Tears were my language of worship and were born out of gratitude as years of hopelessness melted away in his holy, loving, cleansing presence. The tears turned to joy and outward thanksgiving as the truth of my transformation began to sink in. That outward expression soon took the form of song as the words and emotions tried vainly to keep up with all God was doing in my heart! Worshiping God is as much a part of my identity as love is a part of God's!

As I began to share publicly all that God had done for me, others began to realize they, too, could be set free! As God expanded my ministry and others began to be set free, the attacks of the Enemy began to come. I had to realize early on that people were not the enemy—the Enemy was! The reason I share this is because of the assaults I soon came under from people I respected. To be told my ministry would be over if I shared my past openly was very difficult to swallow, yet I had to obey God. But to be told my music was sensual and led people to lust was one of the most hurtful things ever spoken to me. In both instances, though, I had to fight the urge to lash out and hurt back. When I don't have a clue about how to respond to a trying situation, I revert to simplicity: Love God.

Love people. So I began to thank God for the trial and for loving me. I began to declare in song how I had seen his hand of deliverance so many times in the past that I could not doubt him or turn from him now. I worked through the darkness by proclaiming the Light in songs of worship to my God...and peace came.

When God called me to leave Oklahoma City and move back to the farm where I grew up, I had yet another opportunity to praise him through a time of crisis. My wife, Melinda, prematurely gave birth to our boys Asa and Ezra. We had just moved, so we had no friends with us...everyone we knew was two hours away! Because of all Melinda's body had been through, her liver began to hemorrhage, and I was told to pray—there was nothing the doctors could do. Alone. Scared. Hurting. Helpless. So many thoughts consumed me through this ordeal. We had received the news late at night, and I had to call Melinda's mom and tell her she needed to be here because her daughter might not make it through that night...and I felt defeated. What did I do? I began to worship my God. Though the situation was grim, my heart was buoyed by God's presence. Melinda's soul was sustained by his presence. And the Enemy and his lies were put down by the truth. People began to show up out of nowhere to pray, not even knowing the ominous state of things. God began to heal.

Later, when my sister-in-law lost her six-year-old nephew, Jordan, in a traffic accident, she asked me to lead worship at the funeral. His favorite song had been one I had written—"You Are My All in All." Worship God at a time like this? The parents knew Jordan was with Jesus. Though they knew this, they had to bear the weight of losing him, and they desired to honor God. The pain did not go away. But it was made more bearable because God's presence helped carry the load. That load, bearing was facilitated by an open, intimate relationship toward a God who knows and bears and shares in our grief.

I would never make it one day without the Lord in my life. I facilitate that intimate relationship with him daily—moment by moment—by worshiping and praising him. It's natural for me, a real and vital part of my identity in Christ, to worship him at every stage and interval of my life—no matter how joyful, no matter how incredibly painful, no matter how sad.

Though not always the inclination of my weary human body, my true nature is always to respond to the Lord in any situation.

How do people make it without Jesus? I honestly do not know: But what I do know is that I could never make it one day without him...and I do not have to, because he has made a way for me to commune with him in any situation. What a awesome, loving God we serve. We never have to walk alone. With my praise I will know him.

MEDITATION

- What is praise? What is worship?
- Why are they vital to overcoming the old and putting on the new?
- How does the Lord use praise to scatter the Enemy?
- What are some instances in your own Me where you need to put on praise?

TRUTHS FOR MEDITATION

"Whatever was to my profit I now consider loss for the sake of Christ."
—Philippians 3: 7

"Blessed is the man who perseveres under trial, because when he has stood the test, he will receive the crown of life that God has promised to those who love him."
—James 1:12

IN YOUR SLEEP TONIGHT, allow your soul to rest in his presence. Praise God for some trial you are currently facing, and trust him to meet you in the midst of that trial.

"Even in their sleep..."
—Psalm 127:2 NASB

hide me in the
cleft of the rock

CHAPTER 9

Hide me in the
CLEFT
of the Rock

Hide Me in the Cleft of the Rock

Hide me in the cleft of the Rock;
Clothe me in the love of the Son.
Lord, surround me! Surround me!
I release the joy of my heart,
Flowing from the River of Life!

For you are my Refuge,
A present help in my trouble,
A River of Gladness,
My help as the morning comes.
You are my Refuge.
Though the world falls around me,
I will not fear, lord,
For I have your love!

hide me in the cleft of your heart;
Surround me with the pow'r
Of your love.
Lord, surround me! Surround me!
You are like a tower of strength,
Your faithfulness a shelter for me!
Lord, surround me with your love!

For you are my Refuge,
A present help in my trouble,
A River of Gladness,
My help as the morning comes.
You are my Refuge.
Thought the world falls around me,
I will not fear, Lord,
For I have your love!

INSPIRATION

Exodus 33:12-23
April 15, 1987 and
November 10, 1997

WHEN THE ENEMY attacks, whether with temptations or with accusations, either we listen or we fight. When we listen to the Enemy, we actually aid him in placing the old, debilitating weights around our necks. When we fight, we respond with truth, and the truth always has the effect of setting us free. One of the ways we can fight off these attacks is by placing ourselves within the sanctuary of God's presence until the storm passes over. I find this the best counterattack when I feel personally weak or overwhelmed. Instead of listening to the Enemy, I must hide myself the safety of the cleft of the Rock that God has carved out for me in himself. This song was born during one of those times of attack against my identity.

"I WILL REJOICE IN DOING THEM GOOD AND WILL ASSUREDLY PLANT THEM IN THIS LAND WITH ALL MY HEART AND SOUL." —JEREMIAH 32:41

"In the day of trouble he will keep me safe in his dwelling; he will hide me in the shelter of his tabernacle and set me high upon a rock." —Psalm 27:5

"Keep me as the apple of your eye; hide me in the shadow of your wings." — Psalm 17:8

"I meditate on your precepts and consider your ways." Psalm 119:15

A Place in the Heart

WHEN I WAS A small boy, some of my most frightening times were nights when storms beat against the roof of our house. I would cry out to God in desperation for his protection during those storms. When I was older and had sinned, I again cried out for protection— but this time I cried for protection *from* God and the consequences of my sin.

There was a time when Moses, the liberator of Israel, needed protection from God's holiness. He was in the process of leading God's people through the wilderness and had just received the Ten Commandments from the Lord. While Moses was on the mountaintop, the people rebelled, and Moses destroyed the tablets when he discovered the people in sin. When Moses finally calmed down enough to seek God for his next step, he made a profound statement: "If Thy presence does not go with us, do not lead us up from here" (Exod. 33:15). God was pleased with Moses and showed him favor. Moses then asked to see God's glory—the fullness of his presence. God's reply was, "No man can see Me and live" (v. 20). In other words, if we were to see God for who he fully is, we would die from the sheer weight of that presence...the sheer weight of holiness...the sheer weight of purity and love! How would Moses be able to see God's glory yet live to tell about it?

God made a way. He said to Moses, "There is a place by Me [in Me], and you shall stand there [in that place] on the rock; and it will come about, while My glory is passing by, that I will put you in the cleft of the rack and cover you with My hand until I have passed by" (vv. 21–22). God had fashioned a place deep within himself where Moses could experience God's glory and live through it! Could that same experience be available to us today? I believe so with all my heart.

When I came to God in repentance and gave him posses, sion of my heart and life, he transformed my identity. At the same time, he fashioned a very special place for me within himself where I can stand while his presence passes by. My sin made me unworthy, yet the blood of Jesus makes me worthy to stand before God. I have no holiness apart from the holiness of God. The storms I used to fear pale in power when I think of the pure and perfect Holy God who makes a place for me within himself...within his own heart! When the Enemy tries to keep me from approaching God by throwing past sins in my face, I simply remember that my God has made a place within the Rock to hide me and keep me safe and secure from the "ravages" of his loving holiness. I fear God in reverence, yet I am not afraid to approach him anymore. My sins were forgiven—*are* forgiven. My place of protection from the lies of the Enemy is found in the center of the holiness I used to fear.

The Rock God refers to is, of course, Jesus. As my Rock of salvation and protection, I can boldly ask him for protection and security at any moment of the day, even if I just blew it and the Enemy is having a heyday with my soul. I have learned to quickly recognize and admit my sin and turn hurriedly back to God. He is opposed to the proud but gives grace to those who will humble themselves and submit to his holiness. To submit to his holiness is to submit and surrender to his love.

When I am afraid,
    I ask him to surround me with peace.
When I am confused,
    I ask him to surround me with wisdom.
When I am tempted,
    I ask him to surround me with grace.

In each case, Jesus is my Rock...and within that Rock, there is a very special place hollowed out in my shape with my very name written upon it.

It is when I surrender to that place and submit to that depth of love that I see just how precious and special a fit I have in him. When I truly surrender, I find peace in a storm...wisdom from chaos...victory over sin...grace to overcome it.

It is in placing myself in him that I see the shape of my newest identity. This is who I am, and this is where I belong.

MEDITATION

- How does the Lord clothe you in his love?
- What does it mean to be surrounded by God's wisdom? By God's grace? By peace?
- What is joy, and how do you release it even in the midst of chaos?
- What does your place in God's heart look like?

TRUTHS FOR MEDITATION

"Moses said to the Lord, 'You have been telling me, 'Lead these people,' but you have not let me know whom you will send with me. You have said, 'I know you by name and you have found favor with me.' If you are pleased with me, teach me your ways so I may know you and continue to find favor with you. Remember that this nation is your people.' The Lord replied, 'My Presence will go with you, and I will give you rest.' Then Moses said to him, 'If your Presence does not go with us, do not send us up from here. How will anyone know that you are pleased with me and with your people unless you go with us? What else will distinguish me and your people from all the other people on the face of the earth?' And the Lord said to Moses, 'I will do the very thing you have asked, because I am pleased with you and I know you by name.' Then Moses said, 'Now show

*me your glory.' And the Lord said, 'I will cause all
my goodness to pass in front of you, and I will
proclaim my name, the Lord, in your presence. I will
have mercy on whom I will have mercy, and I will have
compassion on whom I will have compassion. But,' he said,
'you cannot see my face, for no one may see me and live.'
Then the Lord said, 'There is a place near me where you may
stand on a rock. When my glory passes by, I will put you
in a cleft in the rock and cover you with my hand until
I have passed by. Then I will remove my hand and you
will see my back; but my face must not be seen.'"*
—Exodus 33:12–23

*"My dove in the clefts of the rock, in the hiding places on the mountainside,
show me your face, let me hear your voice; for your voice is sweet, and your
face is lovely."*
—Song of Songs 2:14

ASK THE LORD to show you the special place he has engraved
in his heart for you.

"Even in their sleep…"
—Psalm 127:2 NASB

CHAPTER 10

Wounded SOLDIER

Wounded Soldier

Wounded soldier on the ground,
Broken, bleeding, beaten down,
Feeling defeated, feeling not needed,
Alone, abandoned on the battleground!
Wounded soldier, faithful friend,
Beaten down by those you defend,
Your heart once open, now pierced and broken,
Needing hope to rise again!

Let me bind up ev'ry wound.
Let me comfort ev'ry pain.
Let me carry you to a place of rest,
Shelter from pouring rain.
Let me hold you! I can be right where you are!
Let me hold you in the shelter of my heart!
When you're weary from the battle and all hope just seems so far,
Just remember I am with you faithfully guarding your heart!

While the battle rages on I will hold you through the night,
I the shadow of the cross I'll be your Champion; fight your fight!
Let me hold you! I can be right where you are!
Let me hold you in the shelter of my heart!

Wounded soldier, you'll rise again!
You can trust me. I always win!
When you face harshness or total darkness,
I'm ever watching, faithful to defend!
wounded soldier, faithful one,
When you're fallen I'll help you run!
With ev'ry testing I'll bring you resting
And say to you, "My child, well done!"

(Repeat Second Verse)

When you feel you can't go on, you be weak and I'll be strong
With the power of my strongest love from my heart's deepest song!
Let me hold you! I can be right where you are!
Let me hold you in the shelter of my heart!

INSPIRATION

Luke 10:30–37
November 4–5, 1997

It is one thing to be wounded by the Enemy. It is an entirely different matter when you have to watch someone you love walk through a hard time of wounding. When I was attacked concerning my faith, my pastor and friend, Chuck, was also wounded in the process. What made the wounding so painful was that it came from people we thought were on our side. Yet it seemed they were working for the Enemy, deliberately trying to cause us to give up in our quest to lead others to wholeness and freedom in Christ. As I sought the Lord for healing of my own wounds, I asked him to let me hear him sing over my heart and to let me hear what he was trying to sing over Chuck. This song flowed from this time of intercession over the course of two cold and difficult days in November. The healing I personally received through this song was worth the attacks we had to go through to receive it.

"HE WAS PIERCED FOR OUR TRANS-GRESSIONS, HE WAS CRUSHED FOR OUR INIQUITIES; ...BY HIS WOUNDS WE ARE HEALED." —ISAIAH 53:5

"He has sent me to bind up the brokenhearted, to proclaim freedom for the captives and release from darkness for the prisoners." —Isaiah 61:1

"Those who know your name will trust in you, for you, Lord, have never forsaken those who seek you." — Psalm 9:10

A Tale of Two Soldiers

TWO SOLDIERS WERE taken captive by enemy forces. Both men were strong and fierce warriors and had put up a valiant fight, yet they were overcome and taken prisoner. One man, though determined to rough it out no matter how long the captivity lasted, was bound by an inner force much greater than any physical chains—he was ruled by fear. His reality was total aloneness. The other man faced the same confinement and chains and the same solitary future, yet he was free from fear, for he had long ago faced his fears. His reality was total fulfillment and the comfort of a faithful companion and friend.

As the days went by, the first man was easily persuaded to believe the lies and the propaganda the Enemy fed him. Soon, his tough exterior gave way to the force of his inner fear, and the once strong warrior was reduced to a groveling, pitiful wreck of a man. He soon became convinced that the cause he had fought for was futile and wrong. He switched loyalties, trading in years of hard work and sacrifice for the brief alleviation of his fears. And believe it or not, his reasoning was simple: At least he wouldn't be alone!

The second prisoner, on the other hand, stayed calm and strong throughout the whole ordeal. Through all the many hours of questioning and verbal bombardment, his heart held fast. Through the endless days of starvation and demeaning ridicule, he never gave up hope. Through agonizing pain and mockery, through the utter humiliation of being stripped of his outward clothing and healthy appearance, he never lost his dignity—and never lost sight of his identity. He had come to the resolve he needed long before the war started, and the truth of the matter was that he had no great strength in and of himself. His great strength and inner peace came from One far greater in strength. And in his little solitary hellhole, there was One who sang him to sleep after the hours of torture. Even in the midst of the countless beatings, there had always been that One, taking those beatings with him. When the days of never hearing another human voice would have driven another man crazy, he found joy in the laughter and companionship of those who had tried to destroy his life.

How could this be? Was he not as "alone" as the first prisoner when their imprisonment began? It may have appeared be! was alone, but in reality, he had been freed from loneliness and fear many years before when Jesus found him and delivered him from sin. In Jesus, he had discovered a love so deep and constantly abiding that he had not only been able to walk away from his sin, he had now come to a place of leading others out of that sin! He had discovered that Jesus, by the Holy Spirit, would never leave him alone—ever! Death was of no consequence to him. He had a faithful friend whether he lived or died. Tell me, if you were one of the characters in this story, who would you be more like?

I can relate to both soldiers. Like the first soldier, I have at times given up. I have felt alone simply because there are not many who publicly declare they have been delivered from homosexuality. But even in such times, God has made himself known to me in some way or another, and I have become like the second soldier. My resolve is to follow the Lord—no matter what. My desire is to so saturate my life with the truth that the lies and failures are replaced with what is right…simply because that is who I am. At those times, I do not allow the feeling of being alone to dictate how I will respond. No feeling will dictate the truth. No feeling will determine my identity. I am free from fear because of who I am.

As a soldier, wounds will come. The war will be intense and unending. Fellow soldiers will leave you in the middle of battle. The Enemy hates that you represent hope to another. He will sometimes use those you trust to betray you. Is knowing Jesus really worth all the heartache? I believe it is with all my heart. Being soldiers of

Christ requires our whole heart, regardless of what the future holds. Why does the Enemy war against you so much? Could it be that he sees something so valuable to God and God's purposes that he feels threatened unless he destroys the object of such hope? Is knowing Jesus worth the fight? You must decide. Only when you decide that knowing Jesus is worth whatever battle you have to fight will your life realize true victory and fulfillment—even in the face of overwhelming circumstances.

MEDITATION

- In what ways have you wounded or been wounded by others?
- What is the purpose of wounds?
- What do you do when abandoned?
- What do you do when those you are in covenant with hurt you?

TRUTHS FOR MEDITATION

"A man's spirit sustains him in sickness, but a crushed spirit who can bear?"
—Proverbs 18:14

"Wounds from a friend can be trusted, but an enemy multiplies kisses." —Proverbs 27:6

"He was Pierced for our transgressions, he was crushed for our iniquities; the punishment that brought us peace was upon him, and by his wounds we are healed."
—Isaiah 53:5

HAVE YOU BEEN WOUNDED? Ask the Lord to bind up your wounds as you sleep tonight.

"Even in their sleep..."
—Psalm 127:2 NASB

Shattered Trust

GROWING UP AN emotional person, I tended to trust in people who appeared more stable than I was—and who would give me attention. But on several occasions that trust was shattered.

Because I was always afraid to be honest about my struggles, as a child I never confided in anyone. But as adulthood loomed on the horizon, I became desperate for help and reached out to someone I believed I could trust. A married man with children, he had a prominent person and great influence in the Christian community. As a last-ditch effort at hope, I finally unloaded the heavy burdens of my heart concerning homosexuality on this trusted friend. It felt good to get all that junk out in the open, and I waited in anticipation to see what God would do. My hope fell to an all-time low when this one I had trusted confessed his desire to be physically intimate with me—and then used me. At that moment, I gave up and gave in to his desires. Why? I felt there was no hope and no way out. The person I had trusted and respected violated me with a perversion I had desired to be free from. My trust was shattered. Not long after this experience, I attempted to take my own life.

After he betrayed me, life suddenly seemed worthless, and I felt worthless. As I turned on the gas and lay down, I began to think about how I would finally be free from my struggles and free from the burdens of sin I had borne for so long. But I also began to think about what eternity might hold for me...and this sense of freedom turned into dread and fear...because I was not sure.

These episodes occurred before I was set free but helped form the basis for strongholds in my life concerning trust, even after freedom came—even affecting my trust in God. After I was set free, my faith and ability to trust would be tested many times. What do you do when you trust people enough to allow them into your home, only to find that they have deceived you and used you and practiced evil in your home?

What do you do when Christian leaders you trust suddenly turn on you and say and do hurtful things to you? What do you do when you are deceived by those you entrust your heart to in financial matters! What do you do when many in your own denomination disown you and try to discredit your ministry?

I have been in each of these situations and have been devastated. Yet God can be trusted—even when his children hurt and abuse one another in the name of authority or love.

When these circumstances occurred in my life, I was deeply hurt. I never wanted to be involved in a church again. My trust had been shattered, and I needed healing. God is faithful and can be trusted. As I continued to seek him for my sanity, he began to remind me that relationships should be based on love. Love requires risk. To have no risk is to have no relationships. I let people down all the time, yet they keep loving me. My wife. My children. My friends. Why? Because they know that as long as I have life, I will be there for them...just as Father is for me. He revealed to me that he could use these hurts to lead me to be a trustworthy man, a loyal friend, and a faithful warrior.

If I can trust God with my heart, I can trust him to heal my wounds. If I know he will heal my wounds, I can risk the pain of loving and laying down my life.

My trust is in God's integrity.
In God I lack nothing!
My trust is in his ability.
With God nothing is too difficult.
My trust is wrapped up in who he is.
My God is able!

When I consider his nature, my ability to trust him and others in relationships goes through the maturing process, a process in which the new creation gains so much healing that he is willing to lay down his life for the very ones who crucify him. This is who I am. Shattered trust? A life made to be broken and spilled out...again and again.

MEDITATION

- How has God taken your mistakes or wounds and made something beautiful of them?
- What is trust, and how do you learn to trust after your trust has been shattered?
- How does your heavenly Father defend you?

TRUTHS FOR MEDITATION

"Trust in the Lord with all your heart and lean not on your own understanding; in all your ways acknowledge him, and he will make your paths straight."
—Proverbs 3:5–6

"I am the good shepherd; I know my sheep and my sheep now me—just as the Father knows me and I know the Father—and I lay down my life for the sheep. I have other sheep that are not of this sheep pen. I must bring them also. They too will listen to my voice, and there shall be one flock and one shepherd. The reason my Father loves me is that I lay down my life—only to take it up again. No one takes it from me, but I lay it down of my own accord. I have authority to lay it down and authority to take it up again. This command I received from my Father."
—John 10:14–18

"Greater love has no one than this, that he lay down his life for his friends."
—John 15:13

WILL YOU TRUST THE LORD and risk the wounds that love brings? Allow him to show you the joy of laying down your life that others might know freedom.

"Even in their sleep..."
—Psalm 127:2 NASB

118

you are my hero

CHAPTER 11

You are
MY
Hero

You Are My Hero

I've seen you standing alone and face the fight
When others laid their weapons down
and headed for home.
I've seen you face the fire and come out shining like gold,
And I want you to know…
I've seen you lay visions down for someone else
And give your life as a sacrifice, no fanfare around!
I've watched you weather storms that would have left others
      drowned,
And this is what I've found:

You are my hero, my knight in shining armor,
A warrior of God's grace, standing alone faithfully!
You are my hero, a light that pierces darkness
With love that's not afraid to fight for someone like me,
Encourage me to stand firm and free!
You are my hero!

I've seen you look down the road and see beyond
The miles and head for truth in faith while bearing a load!
I've heard your anguish cries for grace and watched joy unfold,
And I want you to know:

You are my hero, my knight in shining armor,
A warrior of God's grace, standing alone faithfully!
You are my hero, a light that pierces darkness
With love that's not afraid to fight for someone like me,
Encourage me to stand firm and free!
You are my hero!

I've seen you face death with a deep burning faith
That stirs up the passion in me!
Your heart, like a fire, abounding in grace,
A beacon helping others to see; help them be free!

INSPIRATION

Hebrews 11
February 2, 1997

WE OVERCOME THE Enemy by the blood
of the Lamb, by the word of our testimony,
and by not loving our lives even to the point
of death. When I see others who have paid
the price for freedom and use their lives to
testify to God's saving power, I am blessed.
Part of my nature in Christ is to encourage others. One way I do that is to honor
those I consider to be heroes. This song
was written for those I look up to as courageous and unwavering in their faith; to
those who inspire me by receiving God's
grace through the most difficult of times;
for Chuck, Melinda, Kathy, Terry, and
anyone who is not ashamed of the Gospel
of Jesus Christ...for anyone who willingly
lays down his life or her life for another.
These are my heroes

"LET US FIX OUR EYES ON JESUS, THE AUTHOR AND PERFECTER OF OUR FAITH."
—HEBREWS 12:2

"Without faith it is impossible to please God, becau
anyone who comes to him must believe that he exis
and that he rewards those who earnestly seek him
—Hebrews 11:6

"They overcame him by the blood of the Lamb and by the
word of their testimony; they did not love their lives so much
as to shrink from death." — Revelation 12:11

"I meditate on your precepts and consider your ways." Psalm 119:15

You Are My Hero

As a little boy, my hero was Captain Kirk of the USS ENTERPRISE. He represented passion and determination to do the right thing, no matter what. I would dream about exploring the universe with him every night and looked forward to going to sleep because I knew that my hero would not let me down. But as I grew older, I realized such people were actually few and far between.

A hero is one who walks through fire and flood to do what is right. A hero responds to life like Jesus Christ. A hero...

Inspires me to face the fight when others mock my beliefs.
Inspires me to keep on running the race of life even when
  life leaves me weary and worn.
Knows his or her destiny and is not ashamed to share it
  with others.
Illustrates Jesus in this life.

I have many heroes. One of my first real-life heroes was Christian recording artist Keith Green. I was drawn to his great passion to know Jesus, as well as his great passion to see men and women walk in purity and wholeness. Even though I attained a music degree from a university, I consider Keith Green—from the hours I spent listening to his music—my piano teacher. His message was one of no compromise. He was my hero.

God used the lyrics of Annie Herring to set me free. I was

first drawn to her music because I could hear in it a love for God that could only come from a broken heart. Her testimony to God's healing power ministered greatly to me many times when I wanted to give up. Having come through the pain of drug abuse and the agony of giving up children for adoption, knowing she may never see them in this life, Annie sang of her brokenness and uncompromising love for Christ. This boldness and passion to know Jesus led me to depths of love, forgiveness, hope, and joy that I never realized were possible. She is my hero.

When I married, I had a vision for nine children. My wife, Melinda, did not, yet she willingly laid down her life for me and my vision. Bearing my children and rearing them to love and respect God had already placed her in hero status for me. But when I sat and watched the life draining out of her after the birth of our twins, Melinda's steadfast faith in God sustained me. Hearing her tell God she was ready to be in his presence was both terrifying and empowering. God sustained her life and enhanced mine. She is my hero.

Heroes do courageous things. Terry, a friend of mine, recently felt God's call to move his family from the din of big city life he had known for thirty-two years to the deafening silence of bucolic life in rural America. This may seem like a small thing to many, but heroism is often birthed and forged in the small steps God asks us to take. Terry had to overcome years of familiarity. He had to see beyond the warnings others gave him and hear the voice of the Lord. He had to place his own life and that of his family firmly in faith as he stepped out to follow God. He is my hero.

A hero lives his destiny.
A hero determines to follow his destiny, no matter what.
A hero follows Christ, even if it means ridicule or loss of reputation.
A hero lives in relation to Jesus Christ and is not ashamed.
I want to be somebody's hero.
I want to represent hope and life to the hopeless or those ensnared in sin and death.

Only through taking hold of my God-ordained destiny and walking in relationship with Jesus Christ can I attain such lofty status. Jesus is my ultimate example. Jesus is my hero. I will follow him.

MEDITATION

- Who are your heroes? Why?
- What does it mean to stand alone?
- When have you stood alone in your fight for spiritual freedom?
- Who have you watched face the fire and come out shining like gold?

TRUTHS FOR MEDITATION

"For God so loved the world that he gave his one and only Son, the whoever believes in him shall not perish but have eternal life."
—John 3:16

"Therefore, since we are surrounded by such a great cloud of witnesses, let us throw off everything that hinders and the sin that so easily entangles, and let us run with perseverance the race marked out for us. Let us fix our eyes on Jesus, the author and perfecter of our faith, who for the joy set before him endured the cross, scorning its shame, and sat down at the right hand of the throne of God."
—Hebrews 12:1-2

ASK GOD TO REMIND you of who your heroes are as you dream. Let him remind you of all the reasons they are heroes. See if you don't wake up encouraged and inspired!

"Even in their sleep..."
—Psalm 127:2 NASB

Angels and Other Heroes

HEROES INSPIRE US to know and fulfill our true identity. Heroes encourage us to seek God for our identity. Heroes lead us by example to greater depths of trust and hope in God. Heroes teach us how to receive God's grace.

Think of heroes of the Bible. Think of...

David, the young shepherd who defeated Goliath even though his countrymen responded in fear.

Daniel, who faced lions rather than dishonor God and bow to men.

Esther, who risked her life to save her people.

Moses, who gave up his royal heritage to lead his people to their destiny as God's chosen people.

Stephen, who was stoned to death because of his faith in Christ.

Paul the apostle, who willingly went to his death because he knew God would use it to spread the Good News of salvation.

Heroes face death well. Heroes come in all shapes and sizes. And some of the greatest feats of heroism come in the smallest packages.

One of my greatest heroes is a little girl named Celeste Angel. Celeste is my hero because she was willing to believe God for healing in spite of the great odds against her. Having been diagnosed with a rare liver disorder from the age of two months, Celeste endured years of yellow skin and eyes...years of bumps all over her body caused by cholesterol deposits her liver could not dispose of...years of having to bear the routine emptying of excess bile from the little bag that was attached to her body... years of wondering if God would heal her...years of realizing she was not quite like the other little girls her own age...years of constant pain and the embarrassment each medical exam put her little body through. I watched and listened as Celeste's parents continued to ask and believe God for her healing yet saw nothing significant change. And I was inspired and encouraged to hear Celeste confess that her greatest desire and faith was that Jesus would heal her and give her a new liver. Celeste is my hero.

Celeste's parents, Chuck and Jill, inspired me too. When one was weak, the other was strong. When one lacked hope, the other had enough hope for both. When the stress of watching their little girl suffer brought strains upon their relationship, they laid down their lives for each other and for their little girl. I heard Chuck's anguished cries for God's grace when the healing never came, and I was inspired by his humility and stubborn, steadfast faith in the midst of such hopelessness. I was further humbled and inspired to watch and hear Chuck, my pastor and friend, defend me against the attacks of others even in the midst of all his trials with Celeste. Standing by me when others did not, Chuck had proven his place as my hero. Watching them walk through this fiery trial with their daughter made me proud to know Chuck and Jill.

As heroes often do, the Angel family had already decided in their hearts they would follow God and trust him concerning the healing of Celeste. Their conviction? In death or in life, Celeste is the Lord's, and grace would be poured out upon them no matter what the final outcome might be. Heroes trust God in life. Heroes trust God in death.

My ultimate hero—God Almighty—proved himself strong, capable, trustworthy, and able in the life of the Angel family soon after Celeste's seventh birthday. I remember well the frantic call from Jill telling us a new liver had been provided for Celeste. I remember well the hundred-miles-per-hour race to Oklahoma City that Melinda and I took as we followed Chuck and Jill and their family to the hospital. I remember well the songs we sang and the prayers we prayed during the twelve hours of surgery. And I remember seeing little Celeste's eyes the next day and realizing they were not brown as I had thought all along but were as blue as the ocean is deep! What joy filled my soul as my little hero told me herself that God had given her a new liver. How inspired I was by God's goodness and grace. How I wanted to be able to withstand the same kind of fire with the same kind of faith as this little girl. How I praised God for proving himself once again my hero.

MEDITATION

- Who have you seen walk through dark circumstances yet rely on God?
- What heroes have you seen lay down visions for someone else?
- How have you been inspired by the storms you have watched others weather?

TRUTHS FOR MEDITATION

"My sheep listen to my voice; I know them, and they follow me. I give them eternal life, and they shall never perish; no one can snatch them out of my hand."
—John 10:27–28

"Now faith is being sure of what we hope for and certain of what we do not see. This is what the ancients were commended for. By faith we understand that the universe was formed at God's command, so that what is seen was not made out of what was visible. and without faith it is impossible to please God, because anyone who comes to him must believe that he exists and that he rewards those who earnestly seek him."
—Hebrews 11:1–3;6

"The Lord is my shepherd, I shall not be in want. He makes me lie down in green pastures, he leads me beside quiet waters, he restores my soul. He guides me in paths of righteousness for his name's sake."
—Psalm 23:1–3

ASK THE LORD to inspire you as you sleep by reminding you of men and women of faith who walked through dark or difficult circumstances yet followed after God.

"Even in their sleep..."

—Psalm 127:2 NASB

A Hero's Passion

GOD HAS INSTILLED in his children, you and me, the heart of a hero. The heart of a hero is one that bums passionately for the object of his or her love. To me, passion is a love in which life is less important than the object of one's love or passion. As Jesus demonstrated his passion for me, so I demonstrate my passion for him.

Heroes encourage us in our faith. They remind us that God uses people just like you and me to accomplish his purposes...and they remind us that we have a real enemy in Satan, who seeks to keep us from enjoying and walking fully in our true identity in this life.

The lies I believed while growing up are quite shameful. I can't believe I even thought some of the things I thought! But as I allow Father to speak truth into my life, those lies become painfully apparent now. For instance, I honestly found it difficult to believe my parents loved me when I was young. Looking back, it's obvious they sacrificed for me in so many ways. Besides Daddy's regular job, he also did the never-ending chores that come with running a farm. In spite of this, my dad attended all my basketball games. I honestly cannot remember a single game that he did not attend. What does that demonstrate to me now? That my dad not only provided for us by working hard, but he also put aside his own preferences to relax or to catch up on his rest to be with me. I call that sacrificial love. This sacrificial love makes my dad a hero!

My mom was no different. She, too, worked two jobs. By day she was the school secretary, always available to me—and by night she was a full-time housekeeper-mom-farmhand! When I think of sacrificial giving and laying down of one's life, my mother comes quickly to mind. I recall how she made our money stretch. As a child I did not appreciate her little sacrifices of nice things. As an adult and a parent myself, I can easily empathize with what she gave up for us. A prime example of her giving heart was the time she went to the bank to borrow money, knowing she would have to work extra jobs (like cleaning houses or working in the stockyard office on weekends) just to repay the loan. What was the loan for? Toys for her little boys. I can still remember the joy of seeing the little plastic farm animals and army men fall to the floor as I excitedly released them from their plastic confinements! Seeing the joy my own children receive when I bless them gives me a deep respect for the satisfaction and fulfillment this must have given my mother. To see her sacrifice now, to relive those special moments in my memory, places her in hero status as well.

My parents' sacrifices continue to bless my life and enhance their place in my heart. Because they gave of themselves, I am now able to put down so many lies and to put on the reality, the power, the joy, and the victory of my own destiny!

I have other heroes whom I see as God's signs that he loves me. Take Kathy, for instance. Many years ago, impressionable and needing someone to guide my life, I had fallen prey to Enemy by readily trusting anyone who appeared spiritually superior or more authoritative than I. As a result, I gave up my will, not to the will of God, but to the will of others. As I blindly followed, Kathy and her husband, Doug, often warned me hear God for myself. Kathy and Doug patiently waited for me to obey God rather than people—to walk in my own identity rather than in what others told me my identity should be. This couple fought the Enemy for me, believing in me and my ministry when others did not. They stood with me and looked beyond the words of the nay sayers and spoke truth to me. Had it not been for people like Doug and Kathy, you might not be reading this book right now.

A hero's passion is to see others blessed and set free. A hero's passion was what sent Jesus to the cross. His love for me burned so brightly that he was consumed with passion for me.

It takes a hero to lead someone out of bondage.
It takes a hero to…
    love a prodigal son.
    speak the truth when lies abound.
    remind us that we serve the greatest hero of all.
Jesus Christ is the ultimate hero: He is…
    the One who sacrificed everything to purchase me and my
        new identity.
    the great Bondage Breaker.
    the patient Father.
    the Lie Crusher.
    the Redeemer.
    the Lord Jesus Christ.

MEDITATION

- Who are some of your unsung heroes?
- What lies have kept you from seeing the truth about those who have helped shaped your present identity?
- How does the recognition of sacrifice and bravery in others affect your life?
- What does this tell you about your own identity and destiny in Christ?

TRUTHS FOR MEDITATION

"The thief comes only to steal and kill and destroy; I have come that they may have life, and have it to the full. I am the good shepherd. The good shepherd lays down his life for the sheep."
—John 10:10–11

GO TO SLEEP TONIGHT thanking God for all those he has used to bring you to this place of destiny in your life. Thank him for your heroes, and ask him to bless them.

"*Even in their sleep...*"

—Psalm 127:2 NASB

run the race

Race

CHAPTER 12

Run
THE
Race

Run the Race

Run the race with all your might;
Keep your eyes on the sight
Of my face!
Though you fall, you're not done;
just get up and keep running
The race!

Keep your eyes on the goal.
I am strength for your soul
By my grace!
Through the fire, like shining gold,
Run the race 'til you behold
My embrace!

This race is not over until it is done.
Though fallen or weary,
I've already won!
just get right up, keep running
As if for your life!
Don't look back, just keep your eyes
Here on the Light!

Run the race with all your might;
Keep your eyes on the sight
Of my face!
Though you fall, you're still not done;
Just get up and keep running
The race!

INSPIRATION

Psalm 27:9
July 19, 1996

Each time God allows me to hose a worship conference, I seek his heart for songs to encourage that particular group of people. As I sang my prayer to God about an upcoming conference, I was led to sing from God's point of view. The words for this song flowed out as I tried to tap into what Father was trying to say to this particular group. What came out was simply his truth as derived from his written Word—a song of encouragement.

"HE HOLDS VICTORY IN STORE FOR THE UPRIGHT, HE IS A SHIELD TO THOSE WHOSE WALK IS BLAMELESS."
—PROVERBS 2:7

"For the Lord your God is the one who goes with you to fight for you against your enemies to give you victory." —Deuteronomy 20:4

"Let us throw off everything that hinders and the sin that so easily entangles, and let us run with perseverance the race marked out for us." — Hebrews 12:1

"I meditate on your precepts and consider your ways." Psalm 119:15

When I Fall

ONE OF THE MOST inspiring moments of the movie *Chariots of Fire* was when Eric Liddel, missionary and runner, was competing in an Olympic qualifying race...and fell! The fall was not inspiring, but Eric's response to it was. As he fell to the ground, I could see other runners passing him by. My heart sank because I was sure Eric's race was over now and that he would be defeated. What happened next was nothing short of miraculous—and nothing short of profoundly life changing for me. Instead of hanging his head in shame and defeat, Eric jumped up and sprinted toward the finish line. Resolved and determined, he passed the other runners one by one until he crossed the finish line first! Though he had fallen, he still won the race! That determination, I believed, was in his heart long before he ever entered the race. His determination was to finish, no matter what. In finishing—even after we fall—we win. Eric Liddel won in my eyes whether he crossed the line first or not, simply because he did not give up.

At that moment, my life was deeply challenged: God had called me to be someone brand-new, and my life of newness was like a race toward Jesus, the goal of my highest calling. Along the way, the Enemy tries to trip me up through deceit and manipulation. Along me way, I misjudge the course or make a wrong turn or trip up, simply by not following the advice of my Coach! God's Word compares us to runners running a race of endurance. Our goal, our final destination, is Jesus Christ. We, like Eric Liddel, must determine ahead of time what we will do when we fall (see Mic. 7: 8). Will we get up and keep running toward the finish line, or will we give up in defeat and never know for sure what our destiny might have been?

I determined at that moment that the Enemy would not win—ever—in my life. I have moments when I feel like giving up… but because I have predetermined that the goal of knowing Christ is worth the effort, God's strength helps me up and pushes me off. At times I have felt so emotionally crippled that I could not even lift my spiritual legs…but because I do not run the race alone, my God has picked me up and carried me during those times. At times I have made wrong turns…but because I knew the faithfulness of my God, I have simply reevaluated my position, and through the instruction of my Endurance Coach—the Holy Spirit—I have been able to get back on track and keep running. At times I have fallen due to sin and have felt ashamed and defeated…but because I knew the forgiveness and grace of Father, I have gotten right back up and turned my eyes toward him in surrender and run toward him as if my life depended upon it!

Because of who I am and whose I am, there has never been any doubt in my mind that I would not endure. When Jesus endured suffering and death for me on the cross and then offered me a life of abundance simply through believing in him, I could not help but live my life the same way. As Jesus endured the cross for me, I can endure the circumstances of life for him.

Life is a race, but not one of constant sorrow or suffering. Those are simply little bumps in the road. We do not have to go back to the starting line just because we fall. The race does not start over. We must simply learn to get up and keep running, no matter what.

The joy is in knowing that the One we run toward also runs with us! We are never alone. I listen for him to say things like, "Good job, son!" "Keep running!" "Let's go this way! The view is awesome here!" "You can do it, son!" "I believe in you!"

Knowing he is there shouting encouragement goes a long way in strengthening me and filling me with enduring power. Seeing his endurance and love for me makes me want to get up and keep running, no matter how hard my fall may be.

Knowing Jesus is life.
Life is knowing Jesus.
Experiencing his love gives me strength to keep running.
Running the race is a joy because I know that in the end, I
   win!

MEDITATION

- What goals should you keep your eyes on?
- What do you do when you feel you cannot see the purpose in
   running anymore?
- Where do you look when you lose faith?
- What characteristics of those who have endured hardships have
   inspired you to do the same?

TRUTHS FOR MEDITATION

*"Do not gloat over me, my enemy! Though I have
fallen, I will rise. Thought I sit in darkness, the Lord
will be my light."*
—Micah 7:8

*"Do you not know that in a race all the runners run,
but only one gets the prize? Run in such a way as to
get the prize."*
—1 Corinthians 9:24

WHAT STAGE OF THE RACE are you currently in? Ask the Holy
Spirit to recharge your spirit as you sleep so that you might awaken
refreshed and ready to run!

"Even in their sleep..."
—Psalm 127:2 NASB

I've Already Won

Y EARS AGO, the Lord called me to lay down my life in the area of music. Because I had certain convictions, I could not operate in the music business in the "normal" ways. I could not sell my soul for the sake of a recording contract! This meant that I would not be given me same regard as those who choose to operate otherwise. Please know that I do not believe everyone else sells out just to get a recording contract. Not everyone has the same convictions. That does not make their ministry or calling any less valuable man mine. My race is just along a little different path. Would I give up me race or me dream just because people told me it could not be done? No way! I ran the race simply because God called me to it. I began recording and publishing my own music. If people wanted it, then I would make it available. As I learned more with each recording, God provided a way to get it into people's hands. Soon, God handed me a recording contract. I believe that because I was faithful to run me race God had called me to—in spite of the nay sayers—he directed the race. My desire to run that race was made doubly satisfying because I discovered others in the music industry who shared my heart and vision...and who would allow me to run the race God had called me to without either of us compromising our identities.

In the early days, when I was recording my albums on a four-track cassette recorder and publishing my musical lead sheets on a basic, no-frills Macintosh, I easily could have given up. Generic packaging looked undesirable compared to four-color processing I saw in the bookstores. Yet as the tapes went out and people's lives were touched, an amazing thing began to happen. One person would tell another about the music and how God had used it. That person would then call and ask for it. They would then tell another person, and the chain would begin all over again. Soon, that little recording was in the hands of more than sixty thousand people without the benefit of a recording contract or any distribution whatsoever!

By simply obeying God, I had already won the race, before I even sold my first copy!

Sometimes, your endurance is strengthened by those who run the race with you as well as by those who cheer you on. We runners share many things in common. We all must face the reality of sin and temptations. When I grow tired of running the race, I am encouraged to know others struggle along with me. That camaraderie goes a long way toward helping me endure and resist temptations.

At other times, I must face struggles seemingly alone. My own deliverance from homosexuality and me stigmas surrounding such a race often leave me feeling alone. Yet I can endure when I hear my friend Paul cheering me on like a big brother cheers for his little brother—not running the race for him but seeing the results with him! I can endure when I hear Kathy applauding me from the sidelines with, "Way to go, brother!" I can endure when Chuck calls just to say he's standing with me and that he's proud of me. I can endure when my wife tells me she believes in me. I can endure when I hear the heart and voice of my heavenly Father through the hearts and lives of those who cheer me on. Hearing such affirmation makes me realize I have already won!

A good friend of mine, Brenda, is a petite, normal, hard, working mother of five. Brenda had a vision for competing in a marathon. She could not have done it had she not believed she could. She could not have done it had she not had a goal. She could not have done it had her husband and friends not been there cheering her on. Brenda ran in the New York Marathon and finished. But I say Brenda had already won the race the moment she took her first step.

Long-distance runners have already decided to finish the race—win or lose. They endure the pain and harsh reality of the race and see it through to the end. They run with the satisfaction that the race will be a complete victory, no matter in what place they finish.

I run toward Jesus. He has already sealed my identity by his redeeming blood. I have already won—no matter when I finish the race. The point is that I will finish, and I have already won.

This truth invigorates me to keep on keeping on...
    even when my body or soul is wracked with pain.
    even when others mock me or the One I pursue.
    even when others tell me the race is not worthwhile.
I have already tasted victory.
I have already crossed the finish line a champion in Jesus.
I can endure because I have already won.

MEDITATION

- How do you run a race well?
- What is endurance and how do you get it?
- How do you run even when wounded or weary?
- How would you respond if you were running for your life?

TRUTHS FOR MEDITATION

"The high priest and all his associates, who were members of the party of the Sadducees, ...arrested the apostles and put them in the public jail. but during the night an angel of the Lord opened the doors of the jail and brought them out. 'Go, stand in the temple courts,' he said, 'and tell the people the full message of this new life.' At daybreak they entered the temple courts, as they had been told, and began to teach the people. When the high priest and his associates arrived, they called together the full assembly of the elders of Israel and sent to the jail for the apostles. But...the officers did not find them there. So they went back and reported, 'We found the jail securely locked, with the guards standing at the doors; but when we opened them, we found no one inside.' On hearing this report, the captain of the temple guard and the chief priests were puzzled, wondering what would come of this. Then someone came and said, 'Look! The men you put in jail are standing in the temple courts teaching the people.' At that, the captain went with his officers and

brought the apostles.... Having brought the apostles,
they made them appear before the Sanhedrin to be
questioned by the high priest. 'We gave you strict
orders not to teach in this name,' he said. 'Yet you
have filled Jerusalem with your teaching and are
determined to make us guilty of this man's blood.'
Peter and the other apostles replied: 'We must obey
God rather than men! The God of our fathers raised
Jesus from the dead—whom you had killed by
hanging him on a tree. God exalted him to his own
right hand as Prince and Savior that he might give
repentance and forgiveness of sins to Israel. We are
witnesses of these things, and so is the Holy Spirit,
whom God has given to those who obey him.'"
—Acts 5:17–32

As you rest, envision the day you finish the race of life and
how it will feel to run into the arms of Jesus.

"Even in their sleep..."
—Psalm 127:2 NASB

CHAPTER 13

Love is
WORTH
Living for

Love is Worth Living For

When I first knew you and first love's fire
Burned hot within me, there was not anything
You could ask of me I would not do for you.
But soon my love had grown cold an dI could not see
How far I'd drifted from you.
When I first knew you and freedom came like new life in me,
I knew I'd tasted what I'd been looking for
The moment love broke through!
Don't let me ever forget what I found in you
When you made my heart brand-new!

(Chorus)
If love is worth living for, then love is worth dying for!
It means freedom! Walking in freedom!
        Ev'ry day a little more free!
If love is worth living for, then love is worth dying for!
It means freedom! Walking in freedom! Deeper in intimacy…
In love with the King…I'm free!

Love turns to passion, remembering my life before you.
Hopeless and empty and lonely deep inside—
        no other love satisfied.
They promised me the world, but really they used me up,
And then they cast me aside!
Now I know passion, the kind of love most satisfying,
The kind of love that laid down his very life
        and shed redeeming blood.
Jesus, your love for me is a burning fire!
        And you are my heart's desire!

(Repeat Chorus)

If love is worth living for, then love is worth dying for!
It means freedom! Walking in freedom!
        Ev'ry day a little more free!
If love is worth living for, then love is worth dying for!
It means freedom! Walking in freedom! Deeper in intimacy…
In love with the King…I'm free!

INSPIRATION

Philippians 1:21
September 21, 1995

In SEPTEMBER OF 1995, Chuck Angel and I went to see the movie *Braveheart*. Based on the life of Sir William Wallace, a man who lived in thirteenth-century Scotland during a time of English domination, this movie clearly portrays the truth that living without freedom is not really living at all. Sir William lived his life in pursuit of freedom, calling others to see the need for that freedom. With his dying breath, his cry was "Freedom!" Walking alone to my car after the movie, I was overwhelmed with tremendous loneliness. As I drove home, I began to week and did not know why...and I could not stop. I asked God why I was so affected by this movie. He spoke to my heart, saying that my life is just like Sir William Wallace's. I have been led to call men to their freedom, and in doing so my very life could be required. He said that my freedom is not only worth living for, but it's worth dying for as well. To live is to know Christ, but to die would give me total freedom to know him even more intimately than this life allows. When I got home from the movie, I went straight to my piano keyboard, and this song was birthed as I thought about my life and God's grace to live it well...and on day to die well.

"Be joyful in hope, patient in affliction, faithful in prayer."
—Romans 12:12

"You died, and your life is now hidden with Christ God." —Colossians 3:3

"I meditate on your precepts and consider your ways." Psalm 119:15

"It has been granted to you on behalf of Christ not only to believe on him, but also to suffer for him."
— Philippians 1:29

The Inquisition

THE EVENING I FONDLY remember as the "Inquisition" began well enough. It occured early in my public ministry, when God had first led me to share my deliverance so that others might receive hope. Now I found myself in the awkward position of having to explain to an elder board why I should share my testimony when there was "no need" at their church. I had been invited there to share my heard and ministry, my music, with their church. Upon my arrival, I was informed we would be having dinner and an informal gathering at an elder's home. I thought nothing of this until, after the meal, we were ushered into a room where I was placed in the center then surrounded by the church leadership. The questions began immediately.

"How long have you been sharing publicly?"

"Do you always share?"

"How do people respond when you share?"

Most of the questions were harmless enough. The point of the inquisition was brought home, though, by a loaded question followed by a very telling statement: "Why do you have to share your testimony? We do not have anyone struggling with that in our body."

My answer: "Sir, if I shared my redemption and then gave an altar call, you would not have enough people to minister to all the needs." On the following Sunday, that statement rang true. I shared. The hurting came. There were not enough ministers. The huge response told me that though we may not share exactly the same failures, we have all sinned and have all been wounded to some degree by the ravages of sin.

Why do I share my testimony? For several reasons. When God gave me the gift of life, I believe he coupled it with the desire to share my freedom with others. If I had known there was hope for those struggling with homosexuality, I would have sought it long before I did! I could never withhold salvation and hope from anyone, even though it means the regular sharing of my own deepest wounds and failures. Like Jesus, I was called to lay down my life and my reputation that others might see what redemption looks like. Those who flooded the altar that day were not all struggling with homosexuality. They were all struggling with sin...with emotional wounds...with their destiny...with their identity. We all share these things in common. I decided that helping others know Jesus was worth any momentary discomfort my honesty might bring me.

Why do I continue to share? When we find something of great value—something so miraculous and clearly life-changing—we want to share it with others. My own deliverance was like being set free from prison after twenty-two years, only to be imprisoned all over again by the belief that if I shared it with hers, they would surely be ashamed of me and reject me. I knew I was free, but my joy was incomplete because I could not proclaim it. When I decided that it didn't matter anymore how much people knew of my sin, I was set free all over again! Now could run around shouting the truth and joy to anyone who might care to listen. The truth is that I still struggle often with bat I perceive others, especially men, think of me after they realize what I was set free from. How do I keep sharing when faced with such thoughts?

Not long ago, Chuck and I were ministering together in a small rural town. I was inundated with the lies of the Enemy that said, "These men see you as less than a man. They will not accept you as one of their own." As we drove home from those meetings, I fell apart emotionally and began to weep to the extent that I had to pull over and let Chuck drive. As he drove, he bathed me in the truth of who I am regardless of what others think. He pointed out lie after lie that I had believed, then listned patiently as I unloaded the dregs of my heart once again! Soon he turned the truck around and headed back in the direction we had just come from and stopped at a cemetery. As we sat there, Chuck told me to pick out a gravestone and urged me to bury the lies of "what other men think of me once they know my past." And that day, I became a little more free.

Why do I share? I share because knowing Christ is worth the struggle I sometimes have to go through to get to the truth. I share because I want others to know the freedom and joy of knowing Christ like I do—even if it means sharing when others don't want me to...even if sharing means exposing my deepest wounds to the eyes of the world. Knowing Jesus is more important than my past struggles, present discomfort, or future circumstances. His love is worth living for. His love is worth dying for.

Why do I share? Because I need Jesus. Because others need Jesus. I share because the giving of life-the laying down of life-is as deep a part of my identity and destiny as it was for Jesus. This is part of who I am.

MEDITATION

- Who have you always thought yourself to be?
- Is this the truth or a lie?
- Who does Father say you are in this area?
- What must you do to receive the truth?

TRUTHS FOR MEDITATION

"Heal the sick, raise the dead, cleanse those who have leprosy, drive out demons. Freely you have received, freely give."
—Matthew 10:8

"Whatever happens, conduct yourselves in a manner worthy of the gospel of Christ. Then, whether I come and see you or only hear about you in my absence, I will know that you stand firm in one spirit, contending as one man for the faith of the gospel without being frightened in any way by those who oppose you. This is a sign to them that they will be destroyed, but that you will be saved—and that by

God. For it has been granted to you on behalf of
Christ not only to believe on him, but also to
suffer for him."
—Philippians 1:27–29

IS THERE ANY PART of the old you that needs to be buried? As you rest, ask the Holy Spirit to help you see that burial and then receive the resurrection of your true identity.

"*Even in their sleep...*"
—Psalm 127:2 NASB

The Truth About Shame and Guilt

SHAME AND GUILT have been with us since the Fall. In the first days of the beautiful Garden of Eden, Adam and Eve knew no shame or guilt. They were naked yet had no covering because purity requires none (see Gen. 2:25). When sin entered their world, it brought guilt and shame, and they suddenly felt a need to cover themselves. That's what shame and guilt do to us. They make us want to head for cover and hide.

But shame and guilt aren't always bad. Whether they're used for good or evil depends on who's using them. God lovingly uses shame and guilt to correct his children. The Enemy uses the same things to condemn and attack our true identity. Our goal, as new creations, is to uncover the lies of the Enemy and to discover the truth of who our Father says we are. Understanding the roles of shame and guilt improves our ability to give and receive love—with Father God and with other people.

When we come face to face with our sin, we rightly feel *shamed*. We feel disgrace and dishonor and unworthiness. But if we allow shame to do godly work, it will bring us to the foot of the Cross, the forgiveness of God will fill our hearts with hope, and the imparted righteousness of Jesus Christ will replace our cloak of shame. God never meant shame to stay in our hearts; it is only meant to bring us to him. Shame, when left intact, brings a constant barrage against our self-worth and identity—a perpetual onslaught from the Enemy. Shame attacks our identity and tries to keep us down. If our identity is constantly attacked, how can we understand who we really are? Before I understood the healing power of Christ's love, I walked around clothed in feelings of unworthiness, and I thought often of how embarrassed I would be if anyone knew of my sin. I was ashamed.

Shame said to me: *If I am found out, I will be rejected.* The Enemy wants us to feel deliberate coldness or disregard. However, God's convicting truth tells us that God is opposed to the proud but gives grace to the humble. He is waiting for us to honestly accept responsibility for our sin.

Shame says: *If I am found out, I will be abandoned.* The Enemy wants us to feel forsaken and deserted. But God says he will not leave us or forsake us. We are the ones who leave and him.

Shame says: *If I am found out, I will be condemned.* The Enemy wants us to be disapproved of, to be judged and sentenced, to feel unfit for use. But God says there is no more condemnation for those who are in Christ Jesus (see Rom. 8:1).

Shame is a *feeling*. Guilt, on the other hand, is more than a feeling; it is also a *fact*. When I do something I know is wrong, I "feel" guilty; I feel the separation due to the conviction of the Holy Spirit. But there's more to it than just a feeling. When I sin, I am indeed guilty. Guilt is the fact that I am responsible for the commission of an offense. Guilt reminds us of who and whose we are and helps us keep our eyes focused on Jesus. Guilt can have a holy effect upon my heart. Like shame, guilt is good when it causes us to see our need for Jesus. But if we remain in our guilty state, we are left fugitives, fearing, *What if we are found out?* Past sins, when left unconfessed, are like weights if we do not cut them loose. They drag us deep into deception and self-pity, and the miry clay becomes hard and binding. Habitual sins, sins we still battle, are like chains around our feet, and they keep us from climbing into the higher places of God's heart.

Because of the shame I associated with my past sins, I used to shut myself off from others, thinking that living without love was better than possible rejection. Yet all I found in this state was death. To lock out everyone is a lot like the way I picture hell—no love given; no love received. But as I began to open my heart to God's love for me, I realized that it was my guilt and shame that was behind my fear of rejection. Once I was able to deal with my shame and guilt at the Cross of Christ, I was able to open myself up to love others and to receive love from others—*even* though the possibility of rejection remained.

When I was born again in Christ,
   shame lost its power because my nakedness was covered
      by Jesus.
When I came to Christ,
   guilt became a tool in the hand of the Holy Spirit to purify
      my heart.
When Jesus dealt with my sin,
   shame had no more place in my life.
I can now come boldly before the throne of grace,
   because my sin-debt has been paid in full.

MEDITATION

- In what areas do you experience shame? Guilt?
- What must you do to overcome your shame?
- What is the purpose of your guilt, and how should you respond when it attacks?
- What does a clear conscience feel like?

TRUTHS FOR MEDITATION

*"He gives us more grace. That is why Scripture says:
'God opposes the proud but gives grace to the
humble.' Submit yourselves, then, to God. Resist
the devil, and will flee from you. Come near to
God and he will come near to you. Wash your
hands, you sinners, and purify your hearts,
you double-minded."*
—James 4:6–8

*"I acknowledged my sin to you and did not cover up
my iniquity. I said, 'I will confess my transgressions
to the Lord—and you forgave the guilt of my sin.
Therefore let everyone who is godly pray to you while
you may be found; surely when the mighty waters
rise, they will not reach him. You are my hiding-
place; you will protect me from trouble and
surround me with songs of deliverance."*
—Psalm 32:5–7

ASK THE HOLY SPIRIT to reveal areas of shame as well as a
way of dealing with them in truth. See yourself on the other side of
it-with a clear conscience!

"Even in their sleep..."
—Psalm 127:2 NASB

this is my destiny

CHAPTER 14

This is
MY
Destiny

This is My Destiny

All I was I lay aside now dead to sin,
To God alive! Born again into a new identity!
Once asleep to God in sin, now wakened by the blood
    and cleansed!
Born again to be who he called me to be!
All I have I lay aside, run the race to gain the prize
For the sake of knowing Jesus christ in me!
I cannot yet fully see all I'm truly called to be,
Knowing Christ reveals my hope and destiny!

(Chorus)
He calls me child! He calls me to his side eternally!
He calls what once was lost now found, once bound to sin
    —now free!
He calls my holy! Calls me righteous! By the blood redeemed!
He calls me overcomer, crowned with victory!
This is my destiny!

What once bound me is no more! What was stolen is restored
By the resurrections power of my King!
What was old has been made new; lies and doubts
    replaced by truth!
What was silent now resounds, "I am redeemed!"

(Repeat Chorus)

He calls me servant, calls me warrior;
Calls me royalty!
He calls me resurrected one! He calls me his redeemed!
He calls me higher, calls me far beyond my wildest dream!
He calls my heart to come and be all he can see!
This is my destiny!

He calls me chosen! New creation! Trophy of his grace!
He gives me strength to fight the fight and run to win the race!
He tells me he delights in me while singing over me,
Accepting me as his beloved bride-to-be! This is my destiny!
This is my destiny!

INSPIRATION

Jeremiah 29:11;
1 John 3:1–3
July 26, 1997

My IDENTITY IS often attacked when I share my testimony. I shared a lot the summer of 1997, and was bombarded, yet God's loving and redeeming ways worked powerfully in my life. My own life has been a proving ground for the truths I received in this song. That summer was so difficult in a way, but the fruit was edifying. I have an inheritance that nothing in this world can take away, yet I cannot enjoy the benefits of that inheritance if I do not "cash it in." In other words, I have to receive the gift of my new identity and walk in it...no matter how I feel or what I have experienced in the past. Even when I sin, my identity does not change. I simply get another opportunity to respond in truth to my identity and the God who gave that identity to me. He calls me child; he calls me overcomer; he calls me warrior; he calls me royalty; he calls me his redeemed!

Hallelujah! This is who I am, and it is my destiny...who I will be yet who I already am! This is my destiny!

"I WILL CALL THEM 'MY PEOPLE' WHO
ARE NOT MY PEOPLE; AND I WILL CALL
HER 'MY LOVED ONE' WHO IS NOT MY
LOVED ONE." —ROMANS 9:25

"As God's chosen people, holy and dearly loved, clo
yourselves with compassion, kindness, humility, gen
ness and patience."

—Colossians 3:12

"You are a people holy to the Lord your God. The Lord you
God has chosen you out of all the people on the face of th
earth to be his people, his treasured possession."

— Deuteronomy 7:6

"I meditate on your precepts and
consider your ways." Psalm 119:15

If I Only Had a Choice...

RECENTLY, A FRIEND of mine openly shared his beliefs about God's redeeming power with a young man struggling with homosexuality. This man had been troubled by my testimony, even stating that my freedom was a setback to gay rights and the gay community's efforts to make people perceive them as normal. My friend was compassionate as he shared with this man but firmly held to God's truth: Homosexuality is not natural; it is a perversion of the norms God established for sexual purity. (Actually, isn't any sin basically a perversion of something God intended for good?) My friend carefully guided this young man to an important question, revealing a telling desire in his heart. After this man said he had been this way from his mother's womb, my friend simply asked, "If you had the opportunity to go back into your mother's womb and start over, would you choose to be homosexual?"

To this the man replied without hesitation, "No. I would choose to be straight." Do any of us desire to be anything less than good and moral and upright? We could all stand to ask this same question concerning areas of struggle in our own lives. If you could go back to your mother's womb and choose to be the opposite of what you consider to be sinful about yourself, what would you choose? The only way to choose righteousness is to be born again, giving us a new nature with new desires and filling us with God's overcoming power to put down the encumbrances of the old life.

When I was born again, the old me died. Pure and simple. What the Enemy had stolen from me for years was suddenly restored to me and then multiplied!

*J*oy was stolen,
> but joy was restored.

My dreams of a wife and children were stolen,
> but God redeemed and restored beyond my wildest dreams!

My dreams for a full and happy life were stolen,
> but God restored me when his resurrection power flooded my soul and set me free!

Old is now made new.
> Lies are now replaced by truth.

What the Enemy tried to silence in me,
> I now shout from the rooftop!

I am redeemed!

In Christ, we do have a choice. My feelings cannot choose for me. My past experiences cannot choose for me. They used to influence me greatly, but now I rule over those things because I am instilled with resurrection power that helps me choose the things that are my true nature and desire in Christ. I choose to walk in the reality of who God says I am.

God calls me a servant. Jesus said that "whoever wishes to become great among you shall be your servant, and whoever wishes to be first among you shall be your slave; just as the Son of Man did not come to be served, but to serve, and to give His life a ransom for many" (Matt. 20:26–28). We are called sons of heirs with Jesus Christ of all that God is. "The Spirit Himself bears witness with our spirit that we are children of God, and if children, heirs also, heirs of God and fellow-heirs with Christ, if indeed we suffer with Him in order that we may also be glorified with Him" (Rom. 8:16–17). Jesus served by laying down his life. I am a servant with him, and I will do the same.

God Calls me a warrior! Nothing can separate me from his love. If anything rises up and tries to keep me from my God's love, he has equipped and armed me to defeat that foe and to war against the Enemy's lies with the truth of God's Word, the truth of who he is, and the truth of who I really am! Like my Father, whose blood flows through my spiritual veins, I am called to put down anything and everything that exalts itself against the knowledge of God. I take no prisoners when it comes to the Enemy and his lies. He belongs under my feet and out of my mind and life! I am the victor because I follow the victor! (see Eph. 6; Rev. 12:11).

If I could go back to my mother's womb and choose to be the opposite of what I consider to be sinful about myself, what would I choose? In a sense, we do that when we are born again! We get to go back and start over in our identity! What is even more amazing is that at that point we do have the power to make the right choices. We have the power to choose righteousness over sin, hope over despair, joy over sorrow, peace over chaos, life over death.

I choose freedom over bondage any day!
I choose to be who God says I am!
I choose Jesus!

MEDITATION

- Who makes you choices ultimately?
- How do you receive the power to choose to change or overcome?
- If you could start over, what would you change about yourself? What would you do differently?
- How do you live with those aspects you consider to be unchangeable thorns?

TRUTHS FOR MEDITATION

"This day I call heaven and earth as witness against you that I have set before you life and death, blessings and curses. Now choose life, so that you and your children may live and that you may love the Lord your God, listen to his voice, and hold fast to him. For the Lord is your life."
—Deuteronomy 30:19–20

*"If serving the Lord seems undesirable to you, then
choose for yourselves this day whom you will serve,
whether the gods your forefathers served beyond the
River, or the gods of the Amorites, in whose land you
are living. But as for me and my household,
we will serve the Lord."*
—Joshua 24:15

SLEEP AND MEDITATE on the fact that God is changing you day by day.

"Even in their sleep..."
—Psalm 127:2 NASB

Things Not Seen

GOD SAW SOMETHING in Gideon that Gideon could not see. In Judges, we find the story of the Israelites being held captive by the Midianites. The whole nation is reduced to fear and trembling for many years. The story begins with Gideon cowered down in a threshing pit fearfully going about his work yet hidden from the eyes of the Midianites. Suddenly, an angel of the Lord appears to Gideon and declares, "The Lord is with you, O valiant warrior" (Judg. 6:12). Valiant warrior? Wouldn't the term "yellow-bellied chicken" have been more appropriate? Yet when God looked upon Gideon, he saw a valiant warrior! As Gideon learned to walk in his true identity, he was given more and more authority among his own people and eventually led them to overcome all their enemies. If Gideon had not believed the word of the Lord, he never would have walked in the reality of his true nature. He never would have seen the potential of his destiny fulfilled.

How do we put on the truth when our life says one thing about our identity yet God calls us something new? My inability to see what God sees does not negate the truth! That brings me great joy and peace as I pursue him. In faith, I simply respond to the truth regardless of whether I feel like a new creation or not. The truth has the awesome ability to transcend any feeling or circumstance I face. The truth sets me free from the snares of fleshly feelings and actually taps me into the emotions of my Creator. The truth sets me free from the snares of hopelessness by taking my eyes off of me and my circumstances and placing my gaze upon the goal of my calling, Jesus Christ.

As a new creation learning to see myself as God sees me, I must also learn to see others the way he sees them. I can no longer judge people according to what I see; rather, I choose to judge them according to their destiny and true calling. With other believers, I can make appeals for them to put an end to sinful behavior based upon their identity in Christ. With my own children, if I see them sin (lying, for instance), I can say, "Honey, you lied to me, but that is not who you are. You are not a liar. A new creation's true desire is to tell the truth. You are a truthful person. Put off the old and put on the new of who you really are." In that way, we confront and deal with sin, yet we tear down only the sin, not the person. This is how we build one another up. This is how God builds us up! In this way, we each become testimonies of God's grace to the world, like trophies that declare the power of God!

Father says I am a trophy of grace. While this is not a scriptural term, it does express scriptural truth. The redeemed life is a trophy or reminder to all who see one of God's greatest achievements—you! The apostle Paul suffered, yet he believed his sufferings and the display of God's grace had a profound purpose: "That the grace which is spreading to more and more people, cause the giving of thanks to abound to the glory of God." (2 Cor.4:15).

Father says I am a letter, written to all mankind (see 2 Cor. 3:2–3). All the changes God brings about in our lives become a love letter from him for everyone to read! My life without Jesus spoke volumes. My redeemed life reads like a letter that was written with the greatest of care. My desire is that God be glorified for all he has done for me, so I open that letter, my heart, for others to see and read. My desire is that, as they read, their lives are brought to a saving faith in Jesus Christ as well!

What do others see when they read our lives? Will we allow others to see and read, or will we hide what we have experienced of God?

We have nothing to be ashamed of by being honest. Honesty is a by-product of truth. Truth sets us—and others—free!

Let us see beyond our own perceptions.
Let us see ourselves as Father sees us.
Let us see others as Father sees them.

MEDITATION

- What will others see of Father's love as they read the letter of your life?
- What would you like them to see?
- Will you allow others to see your life, or will you keep God's love hidden?
- Are the lives of others worth the risk of being hurt as you express God's love to them?

TRUTHS FOR MEDITATION

"When the angel of the Lord appeared to Gideon, he said, 'The Lord is with you, mighty warrior.'"
—Judges 6:12

"You yourselves are our letter, written on our hearts, known and read by everybody. You show that you are a letter from Christ, the result of our ministry, written not with ink but with the Spirit of the living God, not on tablets of strong but on tablets of human hearts."
—2 Corinthians 3:2–3

ASK THE LORD to allow you, as he did Gideon, to hear his word to you concerning your identity. Even in your sleep, be listening for the truth.

"Even in their sleep..."

—Psalm 127:2 NASB

A Coat in Winter

SATAN IS A VERY real adversary. As our adversary, he tries to erect strongholds in our minds that oppose the knowledge of God, that oppose our knowing God! In the realm of spiritual warfare, a stronghold is a place in our minds where the Enemy has "dug in" a negative pattern of thinking, a denial of our new nature in Christ. While Satan cannot read our minds, he has watched us operate over the years and knows our weaknesses. In fact, he helped us build the very strongholds that bind us! And those strongholds must be torn down. Some come down in the same way they were built—brick by brick—while others we can crash through with lightning speed. We must remember to never grow weary in the process. Tearing down will require energy and work; but we are already accepted by God, and he will help us through the process. And we must remember that God causes all things to work together for the good of those who love him—of those who are called according to his purpose! If you are born again, you are called!

When I went away to college, I had no money. I worked many hours to support myself during those days. That first year away from home found me with no winter coat and no money to buy one! My parents could not afford to help me out, so my mother suggested I purchase a coat on layaway. Many times I felt like giving

167

up and just staying indoors the rest of my life. But the need to go work and to class kept pushing me out the door during those windy, bitter winter days in Oklahoma. Finally, Christmas break came, and I had saved enough money to redeem my coat from layaway. The warmth of that coat was much more precious to me than to those who had not worked so hard for theirs. Those cold memories remind me how grateful I was for the warmth.

Knowing God is no different. Born again, I became alive in him but was in need of discovering the coat of my identity. The harsh coldness of winter's sin had kept me in pursuit of that goal—it still does—because I remember how cold and deathly life without him was. To finally understand the warmth of his presence in my life, I set out on a journey of discovering the depths of just how warm knowing him really is! The journey toward knowing him always leaves me refreshed at every new discovery of who I am. At every place I put off the old and put on the new, I discover just how perfectly Father and I fit. I found a coat so precious I would suffer through the harshest of winters to obtain it. I wear it proudly. I have put on Christ.

But Satan attempts to strip us of our new coats, to erect strongholds in our minds, denying who we are and sabotaging our new identities. When Satan's lies take hold in our minds, we must answer with God's truth.

Who does Father say I am? He calls me royalty. He is my King. I am his subject and faithful follower, willing and waiting to do his bidding. If he is King, then I am of a kingly race, raised up to rule over sin and darkness! (see 1 Pet. 2:9).

Who does Father say I am? He calls me resurrected one. Like Christ, I died to sin and was raised to walk in a new life. In fact, it is no longer I who live, but Christ who lives in me. And the life I now live in this fleshly body I live by faith in the Son of God, who loved me, and delivered himself up for me! (see Gal. 2:20).

Who does Father say I am? He calls me to rise above temptation to a higher plain of existence, to that of a new creation. He calls me up higher, beyond my wildest dreams and beyond where I used to be (Isa. 40:31). He calls me to come and be who he has called me to be in spite of past sins, present feelings, or future circumstances.

Who does Father say I am? He calls me chosen. To be chosen means he purposely wanted me—he valued and treasured me! To understand our value to God, to truly understand the price he paid for relationship with us, is to be set irrevocably free! (see 1 Pet. 2:9).

Who does Father say I am? He calls me a new creation! I am no longer what I used to be—I'm someone made righteous and set free; I am clean and forgiven! I am in the process of discovering just how deep that newness really goes, just how free I really am, just how much bondage I can overcome until I see him face to face! (see 2 Cor. 5:17).

Who am I? I am all he says I am. When I put off the old and put on the new, I find that I look pretty good clothed in the righteousness of God.

MEDITATION

- How does what God says of you fit with what you have believed about yourself to this point?
- What strongholds would God have you tear down in your life?
- Once you have torn them down, what will you put on in their place?
- Describe how you'd look clothed in the righteousness of God.

TRUTHS FOR MEDITATION

"We know that in all things God works for the good of those who love him, who have been called according to his purpose."
—Romans 8:28

"I urge you, brothers, in view of God's mercy, to offer your bodies as living sacrifices, holy and pleasing to God—this is your spiritual act of worship. Do not conform any longer to the pattern of this world, but be transformed by the renewing of your mind. Then you will be able to test and approve what God's will

is—his good, pleasing and perfect will."
—Romans 12:1–2

ASK FATHER TO TEAR down strongholds in your mind and replace them with hold fortifications, even as you sleep.

"Even in their sleep..."
—Psalm 127:2 NASB

Who do You Think You Are?

"As [A MAN] THINKS in his heart, so is he" (Prov. 23:7 NKJV). In other words, I am who I believe I am.

But who do you determine what you believe about yourself? There comes a time in your life when you decide *who* you will believe—when you decide who is *Lord.*

Either you will serve and believe yourself, or you will serve and believe God. I made the decision long ago that I would serve and believe God. Period! Argument settled. Destiny sealed!

What is destiny? Destiny is a predetermined course of event beyond my power or control. Once I am in Christ, my destiny is sealed. Who he says I am, I am! I simply believe in my heart that what he says about me is true. As I think in my heart, so I am.

Who does Father say I am? He says I am his child.

Being a child means that someone else provides for my physical, emotional, and spiritual needs.

Being God's child means that I am not only loved by God, I am nurtured by him.

170

He feeds me, he educates me, and he trains me in his
ways.
He is there at every stage of my development to guide my
growth toward my true identity and nature as
his child.
Being a child of God is to be the most cherished and prized
possession of the God of the universe!

Who does Father say I am? He says I am so loved by him that
he wants to spend eternity with me. Jesus said, "I will come again,
and receive you to Myself; that where I am, there you may be also."
(John 14:3). God loves us so much that he gave his only Son, Jesus
Christ, as a sacrifice for our sins. This gift is free to whoever will
believe on him. (see John 3:16). In Christ, we are eternal beings
called to live forever with our God and Creator!

Who does Father say I am? He says I am found. Though I was
once lost, I am now found (see Luke 15:32). Like the prodigal son
who returned after losing his way in the world, I was the guest of
honor at a party thrown in heaven when I was found. This marvel-
ous party celebrated finding what which was lost...me!

Who does Father say I am? H e says I am righteous. Though I
have no righteousness of my own, God declares me righteous simply by virtue of my faith in the cleansing blood of Jesus. Abraham
was declared righteous when he responded to God in faith: "Abraham believed God, and it was reckoned to him as righteousness"
(Gal. 3:6). God's Word is clear: "The righteous man shall live by faith"
(Gal. 3:11).

My faith in Christ makes me righteous. My righteousness
makes me walk by faith! "For with the heart man believes, resulting in righteousness, and with the mouth he confesses, resulting in
salvation" (Rom. 10:10).

As I believe in my heart,
so I am.
As I believe in my heart,
I confess.
As I confess my identity,

the roots of truth are allowed to blossom and grow day
by day until the seed of righteousness, which wa.
planted by the Spirit of God in my heart, over
shadows any remnant of my old life and identity.

"He made him who knew no sin to be sin on our behalf, tha
we might become the righteousness of God in Him" (2 Cor. 5:21)
Who am I? I am the righteousness of God in Jesus Christ!

MEDITATION

- How are what you think of yourself and what God thinks of
  you different?
- What must you do to come into agreement with God?
- What is your destiny in Christ?
- What does it mean to be the righteousness of God in Jesus
  Christ?

TRUTHS FOR MEDITATION

"'My thoughts are not your thoughts, neither are your
ways my ways,' declares the Lord."
—Isaiah 55:8

"As [a man] thinks in his heart, so is he."
—Proverbs 23:7

"When I was a child, I talked like a child, I thought
like a child, I reasoned like a child. When I became a
man, I put childish ways behind me."
—1 Corinthians 13:11

"Brothers, stop thinking like children. In regard to evil
be infants, but in your thinking be adults."
—1 Corinthians 14:20

ALLOW THE HOLY SPIRIT to begin to lead you into visions and dreams concerning your destiny in him.

"*Even in their sleep...*"

—Psalm 127:2 NASB

This is My Destiny

MY FATHER SAYS I am a *winner*! He gives me the strength to fight the good fight of faith and to run the race for the prize of my highest calling! Though I fall, I get up and keep running! But in order to win a race, I must *run*!

> Do you not know that those who run in a race all run, but only one receives the prize? Run in such a way that you may win. (1 Cor. 9:24)

> Let us also lay aside every encumbrance, and the sin which so easily entangles us, and let us run with endurance the race that is set before us, fixing our eyes on Jesus, the author and perfecter of faith, who for the joy set before Him endured the cross, despising the shame, and has sat down at the right hand of the throne of God. For consider Him who has endured such hostility by sinners against Himself, so that you may not grow weary and lose heart. (Heb. 12:1–3)

My Father says I am a *fighter*! I do not give up—I am tenacious concerning my desire to conquer sin and to glorify my Redeemer. I fight the good fight of faith by taking hold of the eternal life to which I am called, declaring the truth to all who would see or hear—

I am redeemed! (see 1 TIm. 6:12).

My Father says he *delights* in me! Even more than I delight in him! His thoughts toward me outnumber the sands of the sea (see Ps. 139:17–18). Mine toward him come nowhere near that! I do not have to earn his delight; I already have it by virtue of the redeeming work of Christ on the cross. God's Word says he has made us accepted in the Beloved—accepted and approved in Christ! (see Eph. 1:6).

My Father says I am the *fragrance of Christ*. My life stands as a testimony for all to "smell."

> For we are a fragrance of Christ to God among those who are being saved and among those who are perishing; to the one an aroma from death to death, to the other an aroma from life to life. (2 Cor. 2:15–16)

My Father says I am a *bride and Jesus is my bridegroom* (see Eph. 5:25; Rev. 21:9). One day, my truest identity will be fulfilled in the consummation of true oneness with Christ in the eternal glory of heaven. What joy and pleasure to know I do not have to wait until heaven to experience that joy. I am known by my God in a deeply personal and intimate way, and he allows me to know him!

This is my destiny, "that I may know Him, and the power of His resurrection" (Phil. 3:10).

We will be afflicted in this life,
  but we will not be crushed.
We may be perplexed by the twists and turns of our lives,
  but we will not despair.
We will be persecuted for the sake of righteousness,
  but we will never be forsaken.
We may even be struck down because of our faith,
  but we cannot be destroyed!

Why? Because this is part of our identity and destiny in Christ. This is who we are!

Therefore we do not lost heart, but through our outer man is decaying, yet our inner man is being renewed day by day. For momentary, light affliction is producing for us an eternal weight of glory far beyond all comparison, while we look not at the things which are seen, but at the things which are not seen; for the things which are seen are temporal, but the things which are not seen are eternal. (2 Cor. 4:16–18)

Believer, this is your destiny. This is who you are called to be. I am so proud of you! Keep your eyes fixed on Jesus. Enjoy the journey. Enjoy getting to know your God. I cannot wait until we have the time of eternity to share one another's stories of God's redemption. Look for me around the throne. I'll be waiting to hear and testify of God's goodness with you forever!

MEDITATION

- What is your destiny revealed by God as you have read this book?
- How does this revelation affect your life? Your choices? Your outlook?
- What does it mean to be a winner? A fighter? A delight to your Father God? The fragrance of Christ? The bride of Christ?
- How does it feel to be accepted by and approved by God? In what ways have you felt his acceptance and approval?
- What would you like the world to see when it looks at you?
- What are some ways the Lord can use your life to profoundly affect the world around you with his love?

TRUTHS FOR MEDITATION

"How precious to me are your thoughts, O God!
How vast is the sum of them! Were I to count them,
they would outnumber the grains of sand. When I
awake, I am still with you."
—Psalm 139:17–18

"I want to know Christ and the power of his resurrection and the fellowship of sharing in his sufferings, becoming like him in his death."
—Philippians 3:10

"Fight the good fight of the faith. Take hold of the eternal life to which you were called when you made your good confession in the presence of many witnesses."
—1 Timothy 6:12

GO TO SLEEP thanking God for your identity in him and for the destiny to which he has called you.

"Even in their sleep..."
—Psalm 127:2 NASB

LaVergne, TN USA
29 December 2009
168384LV00001B/6/A